John Lennon
The Illustrated Biography

John Lennon

The Illustrated Biography

GARETH THOMAS

Photographs by

Trans
Atlantic
Press

Published by Transatlantic Press
First published in 2008

Transatlantic Press
38 Copthorne Road
Croxley Green, Hertfordshire
WD3 4AQ

Text © Transatlantic Press
All photographs ©Associated Newspapers Archive except those listed on page 224.

A catalogue record for this book is available from the British Library.

ISBN 978–0–9557949–3–3

Printed in China

Contents

Introduction

Born in Liverpool on October 9, 1940, and shot dead in New York on December 8, 1980, John Lennon's life was tragically short and yet remarkably full. By the time of his death he had achieved an almost unprecedented level of fame, first as one of the Beatles and then as a successful solo artist. In addition, John, who had entertained his friends and teachers with surreal cartoons and prose as a schoolboy, had enjoyed considerable success as an author and artist. The rebellious, angry young man had matured into an uncompromising, outspoken political activist and ambassador for peace.

Like so many teenagers of his era, John was caught up in the skiffle craze that swept Britain in the 1950s. After an undistinguished beginning with a band that played at local gigs, he founded the Beatles, one of the most important, influential and exciting pop groups of all time, which played a major role in changing popular music and popular culture forever in the 1960s. From the start, the songwriting partnership of Lennon and McCartney bucked the trend, for at a time when hits were almost exclusively supplied by professional songwriters, they wrote their own songs, and soon began writing for their contemporaries too.

John was never afraid to experiment; his writing evolved throughout the 1960s as he was exposed to new influences, both musical and otherwise. The Liverpool rocker was transformed, via his experimentation with LSD and his flirtation with transcendental meditation, into a psychedelic troubadour. However, the escape he sought throughout his life often proved elusive. He came to feel confined by his relationships, his abuse of drugs and alcohol, and by his fame, although, a frequently contradictory figure, he continued to court attention despite feeling ensnared by celebrity. Perhaps, though, John was most desperate to overcome the emotional devastation caused by the death of his mother, which haunted him all his life. It seems he was forever trapped by that event, frozen in time and still wrestling with his childhood demons into adulthood.

As his first marriage broke down, he embarked on a relationship with the conceptual artist Yoko Ono. Both the press and the other Beatles found her unfathomable, but perhaps that was part of the attraction for John. From the moment they first announced their relationship to the world, they were rarely apart. Increasingly, John focused on projects away from the Beatles, such as making experimental music, art, and film, and he founded the free-floating Plastic Ono Band as he morphed into the bearded, long-haired, peace campaigner of the late 1960s. These changes coincided with the demise of the Beatles, causing the finger of blame to be pointed at Yoko. But the break-up of the band was probably precipitated by the death of their manager Brian Epstein, which ushered in a period of directionlessness during which the Beatles' business affairs crumbled and their personal relationships soured.

When the band eventually split in 1970, John and Yoko retreated to New York, where Lennon continued to experience musical success and also enjoyed a greater degree of personal freedom than had been possible in Britain; despite attracting the attention of the US authorities, John found he could walk the streets relatively unimpeded. In 1975, following the birth of his son Sean, John announced his retirement from music in order to devote himself to his family as a father and house-husband, but five years later, just after he had announced his return to recording, he was murdered, shot dead outside his New York apartment block.

Through a series of candid photographs and comprehensive captions, this book charts the captivating life-story of the complex and enigmatic personality that was John Lennon. It details a life full of apparent contradictions, and the journey that transformed an art-school dropout from Liverpool into a millionaire "working class hero", an aggressive, acerbic youth into a peace campaigner, who, ironically, died by violence. Despite these contradictions, John Lennon was always scathingly honest, and always had faith in his message and his methods. He also believed that on a universal scale, his contribution would be small, but nevertheless, he touched hearts and minds across the world with his art, his words, and his music.

Part One

In my life

The Quarry Men

Left: With the release of Lonnie Donegan's "Rock Island Line" in early 1956, closely followed by Elvis Presley's "Heartbreak Hotel," teenage boys all over Britain were inspired to pick up instruments, form groups, and imitate the sounds of skiffle and early rock and roll. One such group was John Lennon's Quarry Men, which by the summer of 1958 included 16-year-old Paul McCartney (right) and 15-year-old George Harrison (left). John, meanwhile, was approaching his 18th birthday. Having lived with his Aunt Mimi since the age of six, John had been spending more time with his mother, Julia. However, on July 15, 1958, John's world was torn apart when she was knocked down and killed by an unlicensed driver.

Opposite: John with Pete Best (left) and George Harrison (center). For a time John sought solace in alcohol, and both his future and that of the Quarry Men seemed uncertain, but his relationships with college friends Stuart Sutcliffe and Cynthia Powell would prove redeeming. With Sutcliffe on bass and Allan Williams acting as manager, the renamed Silver Beetles began to increase their engagements during 1960, despite lacking a permanent drummer. However, on August 12, John, Paul, George, and Stuart were joined by Pete Best, and four days later, the five-piece set off for a performance-intensive, 15-week stint in the nightclubs of Hamburg, Germany, under the new name the Beatles.

Rocking the Cavern

Opposite: John playing at the Cavern Club. The Beatles returned from their first trip to Hamburg in late 1960, George, Paul, and Pete all having been deported. Following engagements at the Grosvenor Ballroom, Wallasey, the Litherland Town Hall, and the Casbah Coffee Club—which was run by Pete Best's mother, Mona—the band made its debut at Liverpool's Cavern Club in February 1961 (although the Quarry Men had performed there over three years earlier). Situated on Matthew Street in the center of the city, the venue soon became inextricably linked with the Beatles' early success.

Above: Between April and July 1961, the Beatles were back in Germany. During this second trip, Stuart Sutcliffe left the group to remain in Hamburg, where he would focus on both his relationship with Astrid Kirchherr and his art studies. The remainder of the band returned to England to back Tony Sheridan at a recording session produced by Bert Kaempfert, who had previously worked with Elvis. Somewhat self-conscious, John rarely wore his spectacles in public in the early days, despite being rather shortsighted, but here he can clearly be seen sporting Buddy Holly-style spectacles.

Under new management

Opposite: Still making a name for themselves on the Liverpool club circuit in late 1961, the Beatles were seen at the Cavern Club by record store manager and would-be impresario Brian Epstein, who promptly offered the group his management services. The boys accepted, signing a contract on January 24, 1962, before returning to Hamburg in early April. Here they discovered that John's good friend and former Beatle Stuart Sutcliffe had died of a suspected brain hemorrhage the day before—another severe blow to John, only a few years after the death of his mother. Upon their return to England in June, the band successfully auditioned with EMI's George Martin, and soon afterward Pete Best was fired and replaced by Ringo Starr (second from left), the former drummer with fellow Liverpool band Rory Storm and the Hurricanes.

Right: John and Paul were also beginning to develop their trademark performance style, which included harmonizing at the same microphone. Having already toned down their teddy boy quiffs in response to the softer style adopted by Stuart Sutcliffe in Hamburg, Brian Epstein encouraged the Beatles to ditch their rock and roll leathers in favor of smarter attire.

"Love Me Do"

Left: John looking pensive. On August 23, 1962, John married his long-term girlfriend Cynthia Powell at the Mount Pleasant register office where his own parents had wed almost 25 years earlier. The previous day, shortly after the Beatles' line-up of John, Paul, George, and Ringo was confirmed, the group was filmed at the Cavern Club for their first regional television appearance.

Opposite: John, with George, Paul, and new Beatles member Ringo, enjoy a boat trip. In September, the Beatles headed to EMI's studios in Abbey Road, London, in order to record a number of Lennon–McCartney compositions in advance of their debut release; on October 5, "Love Me Do," backed with "PS I Love You," was issued as their first single. By the end of the year, with the song climbing into the top 20, John and the boys began to travel outside Liverpool more frequently—not only to perform, but also in order to record and make live publicity appearances for both radio and television.

National fame

Opposite: An early press photograph of Paul and John. In addition to numerous regional performances and promotional appearances, by early 1963 the Beatles were beginning to gain national exposure, largely due to their inclusion on ITV's "Thank Your Lucky Stars," BBC Radio's "Pop Inn," and the first leg of a tour supporting Helen Shapiro. With support building, the Beatles' second single, "Please Please Me," topped the NME charts in February, closely followed by "From Me to You."

Above: 1963 was to prove a manic year for the group, and for John in particular, with a punishing schedule of performances and promotions, which scarcely allowed him time to see his wife and new baby, Julian, who was born on April 8. By this time, the group had cut its first LP, also called *Please Please Me*, which was recorded in a single day, and went on to top the *Record Retailer* album chart for a record 30 weeks.

Beatlemania

Opposite: As "Beatlemania" spread, diversionary tactics were often employed before and after performances as the band attempted to avoid being swamped by hordes of fans. Here they are wearing policemen's hats in an attempt to avoid fans outside the Birmingham Hippodrome.

Above: The Beatles rehearse for the Royal Variety Show. On August 3, 1963, the Beatles gave their last performance at the Cavern Club, as they began to play to bigger and bigger audiences at larger, more prestigious venues and events. Amongst these were *Val Parnell's Sunday Night at the London Palladium* live television show in October—following which the British Press coined the term "Beatlemania" to describe scenes of hysteria amongst the group's teenage fans—and the Royal Command Performance at the Prince of Wales Theatre, London, in November, where the Beatles performed in front of Princess Margaret and the Queen Mother. It was here that John was to utter the famous line "...those in the cheap seats clap your hands, the rest of you can just rattle your jewelry."

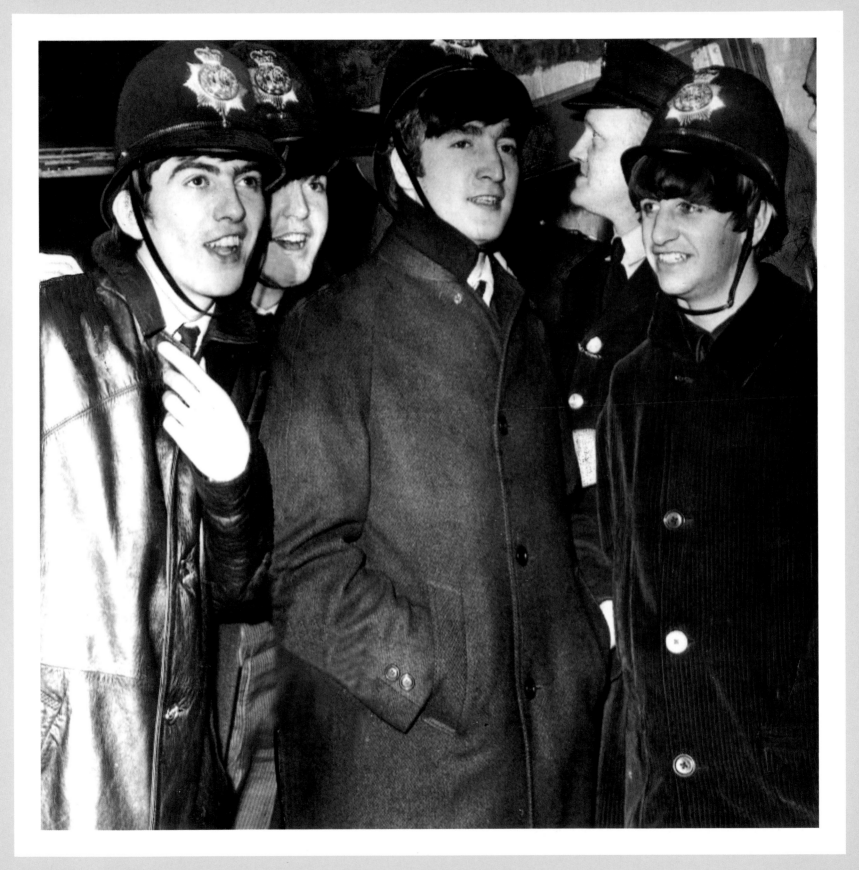

Taking Sweden by storm

Opposite: A thoughtful John waits for his cue. By late 1963 the Beatles had toured the length and breadth of Britain, sharing concert billings with rising British stars such as Helen Shapiro and Cliff Richard, and American rock and roll artists such as Little Richard and Roy Orbison. However, despite this and their previous Hamburg residencies, the band had yet to embark on a proper tour outside the UK. In late October, just prior to their fall tour of Britain, the Beatles set off for a week-long tour of Sweden. During that time, they crammed in some nine performances as well as television appearances, and they were rapturously received.

Right: John and the boys return to home soil after their trip to Sweden, and to perhaps their greatest reception of the tour— both fans and the press were out in force to welcome the Beatles home. Fortuitously, the American variety show host Ed Sullivan had been passing through London Airport at the same time, and his interest in the group was undoubtedly piqued by having witnessed "Beatlemania" for himself.

Chart success

Opposite: John and Paul not only shared a microphone, but also wrote songs together. The Beatles' fall tour coincided with the release of their second album, *With the Beatles*, which had been largely recorded during the summer. Advance orders stood at over a quarter of a million by the time of its issue in November, while the Beatles' fourth single, "She Loves You," had topped the UK charts since August and sold over one million copies. In December, the song was finally toppled from the number one spot—by the Beatles themselves, with their next hit, "I Want to Hold Your Hand." Advance orders for this had exceeded one million prior to its release, but it still topped the charts for several weeks.

Above: The Beatles' collarless jackets and mop-top haircuts started new fashion trends among young people around the world. While the Beatles toured England in the fall of 1963, behind the scenes, Brian Epstein had been hard at work, preparing the first *Beatles' Christmas Show*. Beginning on December 24, the Beatles gave 30 performances of music and comedy over two weeks at the Finsbury Park Astoria, London.

Planning for the future

Opposite: John and the boys put their considerable influence to work for Oxfam, to raise funds for starving children. However, Brian Epstein was constantly looking to the future and had forged a deal with United Artists to shoot the first Beatles movie in 1964, a prospect that John in particular found exciting. He had already expressed a desire to move into movies and away from live performance, and although he remained enthralled with the possibilities of studio recording, he had also quipped that the Beatles wanted "to earn a million quid each" before getting out of the business.

Above: John hesitates over a choice of tasty snacks, offered by Paul. In addition to planning the Beatles' recent British tours, by the end of the year, Brian Epstein had also secured the band a series of dates in Paris for January 1964, as well as a planned tour of Australia and New Zealand to take place later in the year. In addition, Epstein had successfully negotiated three appearances for the Beatles on *The Ed Sullivan Show* in the United States for early 1964, despite the fact that the band was still unheard of across the Atlantic.

Sign here please

Opposite and above: John would later express anger over meeting dignitaries and signing autographs for policemen and promoters—but he was conscientious in setting aside time to sign autographs for the true fans, particularly in the early days. By the end of 1963, the Beatles had firmly established themselves in the hearts and minds of the British public, but they had also been embraced by both the mainstream media, such as the tabloid newspapers and the BBC, as well as specialist music publications such as the *NME* and *Melody Maker*, some of which had previously shunned popular music for its supposed lack of depth and integrity. Despite their newfound success, however, John and the other Beatles were already becoming concerned about the restrictive effects of "Beatlemania," finding themselves increasingly distanced from reality by their celebrity status, expressing annoyance that the music was being drowned out by screaming fans, and experiencing real fears over their safety at some performances.

Making new friends

Above: As the Beatles gained more and more national exposure, and their audiences increased in both size and intensity, a concerned Brian Epstein began to insist that the boys ceased performing in ballrooms, and instead only play at venues such as concert halls and cinemas, which possessed fixed seating.

Opposite: John and George get an armful of two of the Vernons Girls, a musical ensemble of female vocalists originally formed by the Vernons company in Liverpool. Some of the Vernons Girls later appeared in the Beatles' first movie, *A Hard Day's Night*. The boys' newfound fame certainly had its bonuses; in addition to the "Merseybeat" bands that they had known from the Liverpool circuit, they began to forge lasting friendships with a number of fellow artists from farther afield.

A move to London

Opposite: John arrives at the theater, closely followed by a crowd of fans. By the time the Beatles had completed their sold-out run of Christmas shows at the Astoria in January 1964, they had performed to around 100,000 paying customers in just over two weeks. On the 12th of the month, they returned to the London Palladium for another of Val Parnell's live ATV shows.

Right: John and George set off for France—Paul was also on the flight, but Ringo followed the next day, having been delayed by bad weather while visiting his family in Liverpool. Having outgrown the confines of the Cavern Club—and perhaps even the Liverpool music scene—and with so many engagements in London, the Beatles had been sharing an apartment in the city for some time. However, it was around this time that Brian Epstein decided to establish an office in the capital, and Cynthia and John moved into an apartment in Kensington, prior to finding a more permanent home.

Mersey beaucoup!

Opposite: John enjoys a cup of tea en route to Paris. The Beatles arrived in Paris to begin a three-week booking at the Olympia Theater to a rather subdued reception, with only about 50 French fans waiting for them at Le Bourget Airport. Matters improved little during their residency, with performances beset by technical difficulties, and audiences seemingly indifferent to the Beatles' efforts. Unfazed, John was quick to inject some humor on the first night, responding to the crowd's weak applause with a "Mersey beaucoup." Despite the lukewarm reaction of the French, the band later had cause for celebration, learning by telegram that "I Want to Hold Your Hand" was poised to top the *Cashbox* chart in the United States. In fact, sales had already exceeded one million, and their earlier British singles and albums were also set to storm the American charts.

Above: John, with Ringo and George, is greeted by the usual crowds. On January 29 the Beatles made their only recording for EMI outside England, entering a Paris studio to record "She Loves You" and "I Want to Hold Your Hand" in German.

February 1964:
First visit to America

Left: Cynthia accompanied her husband to the United States, but whilst the press had recently discovered the existence of John's wife and child, she was still expected to remain very much in the background.

Opposite: John takes a quick puff at his cigarette as the Beatles prepare to face the American press. The Beatles had always promised themselves that they would not go to America until they had achieved a US number one; by the time of their departure on February 7, that dream had become a reality, with both "I Want to Hold Your Hand" and the LP *Meet the Beatles!* topping the American charts. Although the Beatles' earlier singles had been issued in the United States they had made little or no impact. The way had been paved by the first airing of "I Want to Hold Your Hand" on American radio station WDDC on December 17, 1963, in response to a request from teenager Marsha Albert. Capitol had already been planning to issue the song, so now they advanced the release date, but were forced to contract out pressing to meet demand. The Swan and Vee-Jay labels, who also held licenses to release Beatles material, were quick to cash in.

The Ed Sullivan Show

Opposite: Amazingly, Ed Sullivan almost canceled the Beatles' appearance on his show at the last minute after rival Jack Parr had undermined his exclusive deal with Brian Epstein by screening footage of the boys bought from the BBC. Fortunately Sullivan had relented, and on the morning of February 9 the Beatles recorded three songs that would be broadcast once they had returned to England. That evening they performed five songs live on the show, to a record-breaking television audience estimated at over 70 million viewers.

Above: The concert in Washington lasted scarcely half an hour, during which time 12 songs were performed. As the Beatles were playing "in the round," the set was punctuated by the hasty rearrangement of equipment, to ensure that the entire audience got a good view of the band. Nevertheless, they performed with a rawness perhaps not seen since their days in Hamburg.

Sightseeing in the snow

Opposite and right: Two days after the Beatles appeared on *The Ed Sullivan Show*, they traveled to Washington, D.C., where they gave their first concert on US soil at the 8,000-seater Washington Coliseum. Owing to bad weather, the Beatles were forced to travel to Washington by train rather than plane.In Washington, D.C. John and the boys found time for a spot of sightseeing—which doubled as a photo opportunity for the assembled press. The Beatles were also accompanied by David and Albert Maysles, who filmed their visit from start to finish.

Partying at the Embassy

Above: John waves tentatively to photographers at a party held at the British Embassy after the concert in Washington. The affair began well enough—but after a fan decided to take a snip of Ringo's hair, the boys left abruptly in disgust. They returned to New York the following day, where they became the first pop group to perform at the prestigious Carnegie Hall, giving two sold-out concerts on the evening of February 12.

Opposite: John takes the reigns for a trot around Central Park. During the concert at Carnegie Hall, the Beatles were almost completely inaudible over the sound of the audience, which prompted John to scream at the crowds to "Shut up." Sadly, even press reviews of the shows largely ignored the music and instead centered on the fan hysteria, which had led to the Beatles being shadowed by a large police presence throughout their trip.

Relaxing in Miami

Opposite and above: After the performance at Carnegie Hall, the Beatles had just one major obligation to fulfill: a second live performance on *The Ed Sullivan Show*, which this time would take place in the warmer, more relaxed environment of Miami, Florida. During the day, when not rehearsing for their *Ed Sullivan* appearance, John and the other Beatles enjoyed paddling in the surf and mingling with young people on Miami Beach, particularly the bikini-clad girls. In the evenings, John and the others took in the nightlife offered by the local clubs, and they even ventured to a drive-in theater to see an Elvis movie. John's wife, Cynthia, was still keeping a very low profile whenever the photographers were around.

Enjoying the high life

Opposite: Rehearsals for *The Ed Sullivan Show* began in earnest almost as soon as the boys arrived in Miami. However, they had enjoyed the relative luxury and anonymity offered by a flight to Florida—despite the fact that the pilot was reportedly sporting a Beatle mop-top wig, and a considerable amount of damage was caused by the throng of fans waiting at Miami International Airport.

Above: John and Ringo enjoy the delights of boating. The rounds of interviews and other press and fan attention had eventually proved too much even in Miami, and the Beatles had relocated from their hotel to the nearby Star Island, and the secluded home of a Capitol Records employee, which provided a greater degree of privacy as well as the use of his impressive yacht. Nevertheless, Brian Epstein made sure to maintain the Beatles' profile with carefully selected photo-shoots and interviews, notably with Dick Clark and *Life* magazine.

Rehearsing in Miami

Above and opposite: John and the boys during the three days of rehearsals for *The Ed Sullivan Show*. Prior to withdrawing to their temporary retreat on Star Island, the Beatles gave their second live performance on the show, which was broadcast from the Deauville Hotel, Miami Beach. Once again, the foursome from Liverpool were responsible for attracting an estimated 70 million viewers—more than the entire population of the UK—but, despite this, they were not even given top billing on this occasion; Mitzi Gaynor officially headlined the show. The boys performed six songs, including the massive hit singles "From Me to You," "She Loves You," and "I Want to Hold Your Hand," as well as the album tracks "I Saw Her Standing There," "This Boy," and "All My Loving." With the exception of "From Me to You" and "She Loves You," these were all featured on the LP *Meet the Beatles!*, which had reached the number one spot on the *Billboard* album chart the previous day.

Meeting the greatest

Opposite: Two days after their performance at the Deauville Hotel, which had been attended by boxer Sonny Liston, the Beatles were invited to meet with 22-year-old Cassius Clay, who was training in Miami ahead of his challenge for Liston's heavyweight world title the following week. Although initially slightly reluctant to meet Clay, and somewhat put out by having to wait for him to arrive, John and the boys thoroughly enjoyed their meeting with the soon-to-be champion, and were happy to have their picture taken as they larked around with him in the ring.

Right: John knocks back a refreshing pint of milk. Just a few days after leaving Miami the Beatles' brief first visit to the United States was over, but despite having taken in just three cities in two weeks, the band had effectively cracked the American market, with a number one album, two number one singles, and the promise of more in the pipeline. Almost as soon as the Beatles were back in Britain, they were hard at work, recording their next single, "Can't Buy Me Love," before beginning filming for their first movie, *A Hard Day's Night*.

A Hard Day's Night

Opposite: John, Paul and Ringo on the set of *A Hard Day's Night*.
Produced by Walter Shenson, directed by Richard Lester, and scripted by
Alun Owen, *A Hard Day's Night* was envisioned as "an exaggerated day-
in-the-life of the Beatles" and was intended to capture the "Beatlemania"
phenomenon on celluloid. Filming began on March 2, 1964, and
continued into April. However, the film remained untitled until near
completion, when John supplied the title track.

Above: By now the Beatles were beginning to find themselves courted by
the establishment, with the Conservative Prime Minister Sir Alec
Douglas-Home having recently described them as his "secret weapon"
and Britain's "best exports." On March 19, John and the boys attended a
reception at the Dorchester Hotel, London, where the politician Harold
Wilson presented them with the Variety Club of Great Britain's "Show
Business Personalities of 1963" award.

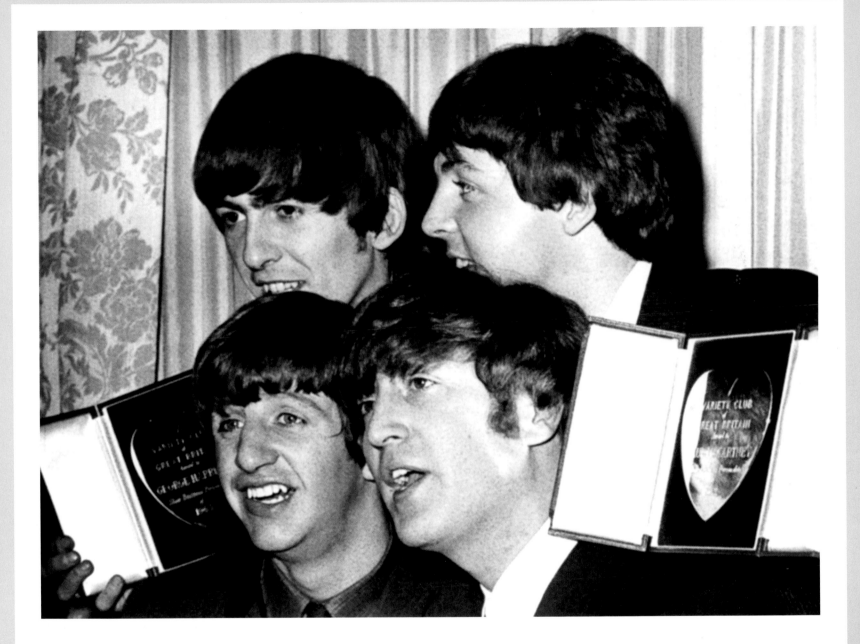

Show Business Personalities of the Year

Opposite: John seemed perfectly relaxed chatting to Harold Wilson's wife Mary at the award ceremony, despite the fact that he was often uneasy about associating with dignitaries at such events and had recently stormed out of a champagne reception at the British Embassy in Washington. Rather than be overwhelmed by the formality of the occasion he seized the chance to make a cheeky remark about Wilson during his acceptance speech, another of his little digs at the establishment.

Above: The Beatles display their awards. George also injected some humor into the occasion, remarking upon the fact that they had each received an award, rather than having to divide one into quarters. Although Harold Wilson took the opportunity to deny that he was courting the popular vote by being seen with the Beatles, he must have been aware of the positive publicity that it would generate, not only amongst his own constituents on Merseyside, but right across Britain.

A busy schedule

Left: John makes his acceptance speech at the Variety Club luncheon at the Dorchester on March 19, 1964. He and the boys had spent the morning filming scenes for *A Hard Day's Night* at Twickenham Film Studios, where they were also interviewed about the movie for BBC radio. They spent the evening being filmed for their first appearance on *Top of the Pops*, which was aired the following week. The show, which had only been broadcasting since the start of the year, was transmitted from Manchester, but due to their incredibly busy schedule, and particularly on account of their filming commitments in and around London, the Beatles were recorded miming to their latest single, "Can't Buy Me Love," at the BBC's studios in Shepherd's Bush, London. The song was released in the US on March 16, and issued in the UK on March 10.

Opposite: John mimes the Beatles' latest single during their second and final live appearance on *Ready, Steady, Go!*, which was broadcast on British television on March 20, 1964.

More awards

Above: John is introduced to the Duke of Edinburgh at the Empire Ballroom, Leicester Square, at the Carl-Alan Awards ceremony. Less than a week after receiving their Variety Club awards, the Duke of Edinburgh presented the Beatles with awards for Best Group and Best Vocal Record of 1963. Around the same time the Beatles were presented with a *Billboard* award, on account of occupying the top three positions on the US singles charts. Within a matter of days they would command the entire top five places, with another seven singles further down the listings.

Opposite: Despite everything else that was going on, John had also found time to write his first book. *In His Own Write* was published on March 23, 1964—the same day as the Carl-Alan Awards.

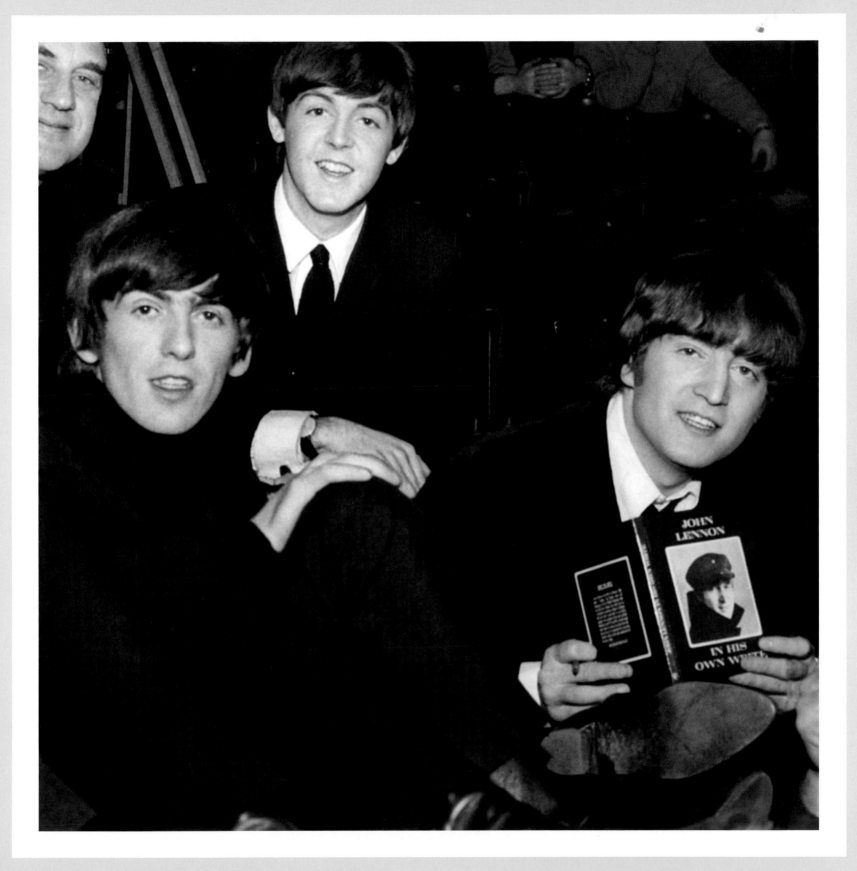

In His Own Write

Opposite and above: John at a Foyle's literary luncheon held in his honor a month after publication of his first book. Encouraged by his mother, Julia, John had written amusing stories and poems—which he illustrated with pen-and-ink cartoons and doodles—since childhood. In his days at Quarry Bank Grammar School, he had created his own satirical comic book, *The Daily Howl*, in which he lampooned his teachers. After the Beatles began to build their reputation in Liverpool, John contributed surreal short stories and other musings to Bill Harry's

Mersey Beat newspaper, and *In His Own Write* was essentially a continuation of these writings, being full of the absurdist humor and wordplay that fascinated John. The Foyle's luncheon was attended by a host of stars, including Lionel Bart, seen with John above, who had first found fame as a songwriter in the 1950s before the musical *Oliver!* propelled him to stardom in the 1960s.

Celebrating success

Opposite and above: John and Cynthia arrive at the Dorchester Hotel to attend the Foyle's literary luncheon. *In His Own Write* was to prove a major success, with its first run selling out almost straight away. However, as the luncheon held in John's honor proved, it was not just Beatles or Lennon fans that were buying in to his talent as a writer; even the *Times Literary Supplement* provided favorable reviews, comparing elements of John's work to that of such luminaries as James Thurber and Lewis Carroll.

Unfortunately, however, John was rather less accomplished when invited to make his speech as guest of honor, disappointing some of those assembled with the simple remark, "Thank you all very much, you've got a lucky face." It seemed that John and Cynthia were both somewhat the worse for wear, having spent the previous night celebrating John's success with the rest of the Beatles.

Double Beatles

Opposite: A thoughtful John, caught unawares by the camera. On April 24, he and the other Beatles completed filming of *A Hard Day's Night*, following which the cast and crew celebrated with a private party in London. However, the following day work resumed on the boys' next project: a television special entitled *Around the Beatles*, which would be produced by Jack Good, and would feature performances from stars such as P.J. Proby, Long John Baldry, and the Vernons Girls as well as the Beatles themselves.

Above: Around this time the Beatles were also immortalized in wax by Madame Tussaud's, and they were invited to the museum for a sneak preview ahead of the official unveiling. On April 26, after a 15-week hiatus, the band made a long awaited return to live performance, headlining the annual *New Musical Express* poll winners' party at the Empire Pool, Wembley, where they performed for a crowd of around 10,000 before being presented with an award by actor Roger Moore. Afterward, the Beatles attended Roy Orbison's 28th birthday celebrations.

A visit to Scotland

Above: John and the other Beatles arrive in Edinburgh on April 29, where they were booked to perform at sell-out shows in both Edinburgh and Glasgow over consecutive nights. Arriving at Turnhouse Airport, the Beatles were warmly received before heading to the ABC cinema, Edinburgh, where they performed two sets, one at around six-thirty p.m. and the next at nine p.m.

Opposite: John signs autographs for some of the fans at the ABC cinema, Edinburgh. For those fans that couldn't make it to the show, just before the Beatles took to the stage for the first of the evening's concerts BBC Radio Scotland broadcast on its news program an interview with the boys which had been conducted earlier in the day at the ABC by reporter Bill Aitkenhead.

Meeting the fans

Left: John meets one of the fans up close. The earlier radio broadcast may have given those at home something of a behind-the-scenes insight, but a few that attended the Edinburgh shows got much closer to their idols than they could have hoped. Having enjoyed an extensive break from live performance, John and the boys appeared to relish the opportunity to meet some of their admirers face to face backstage. Despite his "hard-nosed" image, John, who had always been protective of his two younger half-sisters, Julia and Jackie, and who now had a child of his own, seemed particularly attentive when meeting the younger fans.

Opposite: John and the other three Beatles line up for the photographers.

I tell you, it's this way

Opposite: John fools around with Ringo and Paul for the cameras. The day after the Edinburgh shows, the Beatles were filmed at their Perthshire hotel by BBC Scotland for a short segment on that evening's regional news program, *Six Ten*, before traveling to Scottish Television's Theatre Royal studios, where they gave interviews for the program *Roundup*, to be broadcast the following week. With interviews complete, the boys then headed to the nearby Glasgow Odeon, where once again they gave two evening performances.

Above: On stage in Scotland. There was no let-up for the Beatles when they returned to London the following day, for that evening they were to be found in the Paris Studio, London, recording a bank holiday radio special for the BBC's Light Programme. The Beatles' contribution, entitled "From Us to You," was presented by Alan Freeman and featured eight performances from the boys, interspersed with their trademark witty banter.

Beatles meet Shakespeare

Opposite: John as Thisbe and George as Moonshine, in a spoof version of the "Interlude" from William Shakespeare's *A Midsummer Night's Dream*, recorded for the Beatles' recently completed television special, *Around the Beatles*. Paul appeared as Pyramus, and Ringo was the Lion. The program was broadcast in the first week of May and also featured music from the boys and a selection of other artists, including Cilla Black and Sounds Incorporated (who were also managed by Brian Epstein).

Above: The Beatles introduced the show as trumpeters clad in heraldic costume. The Beatles' musical performance consisted of a set of five songs, followed by a medley of their hit singles, topped off with an electrifying version of an old live favorite, the Isley Brothers' "Shout." The program was made and distributed in the UK by ITV's Rediffusion franchise, but Epstein managed to secure the rights to sell the show in the United States, where it was broadcast by ABC later in the year.

A well-earned rest

Above: John heads off for a well-earned break with Cynthia in May 1964. With the exception of a few days in Florida and most weekends during the filming of *A Hard Day's Night*, the Beatles had been working without a break since the beginning of the year. While Paul and Ringo headed to the Virgin Islands with their girlfriends, Jane Asher and Maureen Cox, John and George opted to travel to Tahiti, accompanied by Cynthia and Pattie Boyd. Brian Epstein did his best to prevent news of their destinations from reaching the press, but it proved to be an impossible task, and the media were waiting when John's plane made a stopover in Hawaii.

Opposite: The Beatles had just made chart history by replacing themselves at number one on the US album chart, with *The Beatles' Second Album* knocking *Meet the Beatles!* off the top spot.

Have another drink

Opposite and above: After a performance at London's Prince of Wales Theatre at the end of May, John and the boys were able to relax with a drink. However, as their wealth and fame increased, so too did their alcohol intake, with free bars laid on wherever they went, and a constant stream of invitations to parties and other social functions. Whilst John was typically charming and witty, he could become boorish and argumentative after too many drinks.

At a press conference ahead of their concert at the Prince of Wales Theatre, the Beatles had announced plans for their first ever world tour, which would take in Europe, the Far East, Australasia, and North America. That evening's concert was one of a series of seven Sunday-nighters at the venue, organized by Brian Epstein, with other headline acts including northern beat groups The Searchers, Billy J. Kramer and the Dakotas, Freddie and the Dreamers, and Gerry and the Pacemakers.

A new Beatle

Opposite: John, Paul, and George fool around for the cameras with some ice. June began with three days of recording at EMI Studios, firstly to complete the music for the album *A Hard Day's Night*, followed by the laying down of a number of new demo tracks on the evening of June 3. However, a recording session planned for earlier that day had to be abandoned after Ringo was taken seriously ill with tonsillitis and pharyngitis at a morning photo-shoot with the *Saturday Evening Post*.

Above: With the band due to head off to Denmark the following day for the first leg of their world tour, Ringo's illness could not have come at a worse time, and the rest of the boys saw no option but to cancel the tour. However, with tickets already sold, both Brian Epstein and George Martin were keen to press ahead, with the result that session drummer Jimmy Nichol was hurriedly drafted in to take Ringo's place on a temporary basis.

June 1964: Setting off on a world tour

Above: Nichol did his best to fit in with the group, both off stage and on, and audience reactions seemed undiminished by Ringo's absence. A night in Copengagen was followed by two nights in Amsterdam. Nichol apparently was staggered by the boys' propensity for drinking and womanizing, with John supposedly hitting the red light district under police escort. On June 7, the band left Amsterdam for London, where they joined a 16-hour flight to Hong Kong, interspersed with outbreaks of "Beatlemania" at every refueling stop en route.

Opposite: John and George give last-minute stand-in Jimmy Nichol an impromptu run through at Abbey Road Studios before heading off for Copenhagen.

Australia welcomes the Beatles

Opposite: After attending the Miss Hong Kong beauty pageant, the Beatles performed at the Princess Theatre, Kowloon, and then it was on to Australia, with a brief, unscheduled stop in Darwin before an overnight stay in Sydney, where the boys were confined to their hotel because of the huge numbers of fans gathered outside. From Sydney it was on to Adelaide, where the Beatles received an unprecedented welcome. As many as 300,000 fans were estimated to have lined the route from the airport to the center of the city along the Anzac Highway—all desperate to catch a glimpse of the boys, who were the first major recording artists to visit the continent on tour. Four shows were performed at the Centennial Hall over two days before the boys moved on to Melbourne, where Ringo was reunited with the band, after recovering from his illness. For Jimmy Nichol this was the end of the line as far as being a Beatle was concerned, and he was soon on a flight back to London, leaving Ringo to complete the remaining dates in Australia and New Zealand before the Beatles returned home on July 2.

Right: Cynthia was used to dodging the fans and photographers with her husband, but experiencing "Beatlemania" first hand must have been a shock to John's Aunt Mimi, whom John had flown out to New Zealand, knowing that she was in contact with relatives there.

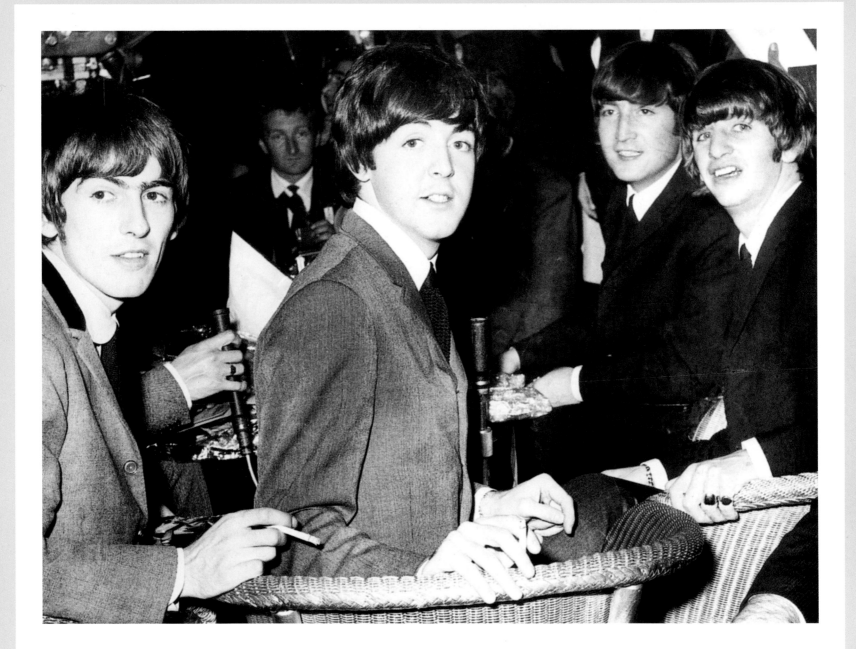

A Hard Day's Night is premiered

Opposite: John, Paul, George, and Ringo are greeted by Princess Margaret and the Earl of Snowdon at the royal world charity premiere of *A Hard Day's Night* at the London Pavilion, Piccadilly Circus, on July 6. Outside thousands of fans lined the streets. Scarcely had the Beatles returned from Australia than the public engagements resumed once more.

Above: On July 10, the same day that the *Hard Day's Night* album was released, John, accompanied by the other Beatles, returned to Liverpool for a civic reception ahead of the city's premiere of the movie. All of them were extremely nervous about returning to Liverpool, but it was to prove a triumphant homecoming—and, for John, a chance to catch up with some of his family.

1964: From America to Dundee

Above: The Beatles on stage in Dundee toward the end of 1964, during a 27-night tour covering England, Scotland, Wales, and Northern Ireland. In September the boys had returned from their first proper tour of North America, which took in 26 dates in 24 cities, including three nights in Canada. There were scenes of unparalleled mayhem, with more than one show almost canceled amid violent eruptions in the audience, while off-stage the boys were exasperated by the media circus. However, meeting Bob Dylan in New York was to prove a highlight for John.

Opposite: John in full voice on stage. In July 1964, John and Cynthia had finally found a permanent base, purchasing Kenwood, a Tudor-style mansion, in Weybridge, Surrey, where they hoped to gain some respite from the fans who besieged their Kensington flat and establish a family home to bring up Julian. However, John had no time to begin homemaking because his grueling schedule of shows and recording commitments persisted.

Another Christmas Show

Above: For the second year in a row, the Beatles were to straddle the festive season with a number one single, in this case "I Feel Fine," and a series of Christmas performances, consisting of live music and comedy. This time the venue was the Hammersmith Odeon, the guests Freddie Garrity and Jimmy Savile, and the show was titled, appropriately enough, *Another Beatles Christmas Show*. The run began on Christmas Eve 1964 and continued until January 16, 1965, with two performances most days.

Opposite: The Beatles pose in costumes for the Christmas show. It was little more than a year since the boys had last performed at the Cavern Club in Liverpool, but 1964 had been astonishingly eventful. Not only had Britain been gripped by "Beatlemania," but so had the rest of the world; the Beatles had exploded into the public consciousness through their own finely crafted songs, had sold millions of records, and starred in a highly successful movie, all accompanied by scenes of public hysteria wherever they went.

Not Only ... But Also

Above: In the early morning of November 20, 1964, John had filmed a number of scenes with Dudley Moore and Norman Rossington on Wimbledon Common, London, for Dudley Moore and Peter Cook's forthcoming comedy series *Not Only...But Also*. John featured in the very first episode, which was broadcast on January 9, 1965, reading excerpts from his book, *In His Own Write*, to accompany the previously shot footage.

Opposite: In early 1965, John reached another important milestone in his life, although this had nothing to do with book or record sales; he simply passed his driving test. Despite this, and the fact that he would go on to own several cars, ranging from an Austin Maxi to a Ferrari, John was never a particularly confident driver, and tended to favor being chauffeur-driven as a result.

John hits the slopes

Opposite and right: Having completed the run of Christmas shows by mid-January, the Beatles had time for some well-earned rest and relaxation, which also gave John and Cynthia the opportunity to spend some much-needed time together. They opted to join producer George Martin and his wife on a skiing holiday in St. Moritz, Switzerland, where, despite appearances, John was to prove a fast learner. By now it was public knowledge that John was married and had a young son, and although Brian Epstein still attempted to ensure that the Lennons would not be bothered by the press while they were on vacation, Cynthia was no longer regarded as a threat to John's image. In fact, on February 10, Cynthia's own fan club was established, which would have been unimaginable just a year earlier when the boys arrived in the United States for the first time.

Ready to film Help!

Opposite: John and Cynthia arrived back from their vacation just in time for Ringo's wedding to Maureen Cox on February 11, having received little more than 24 hours' notice of the event. George and his girlfriend, Pattie Boyd, were also in attendance, as was Brian Epstein, who acted as best man, just as he had for John and Cynthia. However, Paul was away, vacationing in Tunisia, and so missed the ceremony.

Above: Less than two weeks later, having already begun work on their next album, John and the boys flew out to New Providence in the Bahamas, accompanied by actress Eleanor Bron—this time not for a vacation but to begin shooting the Beatles' next movie, Help!. Once again, Richard Lester was to direct, although this time the picture was a fantastical comedy romp which had originally been intended as a vehicle for one of John's heroes, Peter Sellers.

Help!

Opposite: The boys on set in the Bahamas. Whereas *A Hard Day's Night* had been filmed principally in London and in black and white, *Help!* was shot in color, in a number of attractive locations, and although John would later describe the film as "crap," the Bahamas must have seemed an attractive prospect for all concerned, particularly in February. However, it was not just the weather that made New Providence an alluring destination, but the possibility that the island might also offer some respite from Britain's punishing taxes.

Above: Filming began the afternoon after arrival, with John and the boys shooting some scenes in the pool of the luxurious Nassau Beach Hotel. However, John had begun to start the day by smoking cannabis at this time, meaning that for the rest of the Beatles' stay it was almost impossible to film after midday. By the end of the Bahamas shoot, John was happy to be leaving, having challenged the local governor over the run-down state of a hospital that he had come across while filming.

On set in Twickenham

Left and opposite: Having completed filming in the sunny Bahamas, shooting moved to the snowy peaks of Austria for a week, before cast and crew relocated to Twickenham Film Studios at the end of March. The opening scenes of the movie, as well as some other street scenes, were then shot in nearby Ailsa Avenue in mid-April, with John being joined once more by Eleanor Bron. When the film was released, many critics complained that the Beatles were completely overshadowed by their supporting cast, and John himself even remarked that at times he had felt like an extra in his own movie, but off-screen at least there was some chemistry between John and Eleanor, who struck up a close friendship. By this time, John had begun experimenting with LSD, after having inadvertently ingested it at a party held by George's dentist. Although he was initially furious at having been given something spiked, John saw potential for enlightenment in this form of escapism. Unfortunately it increased the distance between him and Cynthia.

A trip to Cannes

Right: After around 11 weeks of filming, *Help!* was finally in the can by mid-May, following which John and Cynthia made a brief trip to the Cannes film festival in France. Until two thirds of the way through filming, the Beatles' second movie had lacked a definite title, with both "Eight Days a Week" and "Eight Arms to Hold You" having been early contenders, until Dick Lester settled on the more straightforward *Help!*. John, who was still struggling with the pressures of stardom and marriage, and who had begun to feel increasingly insecure over his slight weight gain, used the title track as an opportunity to bare his soul.

Opposite: The Beatles pose together on Paul's 23rd birthday.

July 1965: Premiere of Help!

Opposite: During the filming of *Help!*, DJ Simon Dee had visited the Beatles on set in Twickenham, where he had presented them with a Bell award on behalf of the pirate radio station Radio Caroline, and a few days later the boys had been rewarded again, this time at the *NME* Annual Poll-Winners All-Star Concert.

Above: The royal world premiere of *Help!* was held at the London Pavilion on July 29. John attended wearing black tie, with Cynthia on his arm. In general, the response to the *Help!* movie was less favorable, although renowned film critic Kenneth Tynan did not dismiss it entirely, and it later won the top prize at the Rio de Janeiro International Film Festival. John's heartfelt single "Help!" was released in both Britain and the United States just a few days before the UK premiere of the movie.

Hola!

Opposite: Returning from Barcelona following the European tour, John adopted the stance of a matador as the Beatles crossed the tarmac at London Airport, mimicking the pose he had assumed for the cover of his second book, *A Spaniard in the Works*. The book had been published just a few days after the tour began, and its content was in a very similar vein to that of his first book, *In His Own Write*. Once again, as the title suggested, it was full of clever word-play and irreverent humor.

Right: On August 13, the day that the *Help!* soundtrack was released in the United States, John was once again jetting off to New York with the Beatles, to begin a North American tour. However, before he left he had some family business to attend to: purchasing a harbor-side bungalow in Poole, Dorset, for his Aunt Mimi so that she could escape the fans that congregated outside Mendips, John's childhood home in Liverpool.

August 1965: Back to the USA

Left: It was all smiles as John prepared to leave for the United States, but he and the others must have been somewhat apprehensive, having already grown tired of playing to audiences that simply screamed over the music. John may have taken some comfort from the fact that this tour would be short, taking in just ten different cities over the course of slightly less than three weeks, but this time the venues and the audiences were truly huge. The day after their arrival, the boys recorded six songs for *The Ed Sullivan Show* (right), which also featured their old friend from the Cavern, Cilla Black. The following day, they performed in front of a record-breaking audience of over 55,000 fans at Shea Stadium, New York. It was a spectacular event, as documented on film, but John later admitted that he hadn't bothered playing the right chords because no one could hear his guitar anyway.

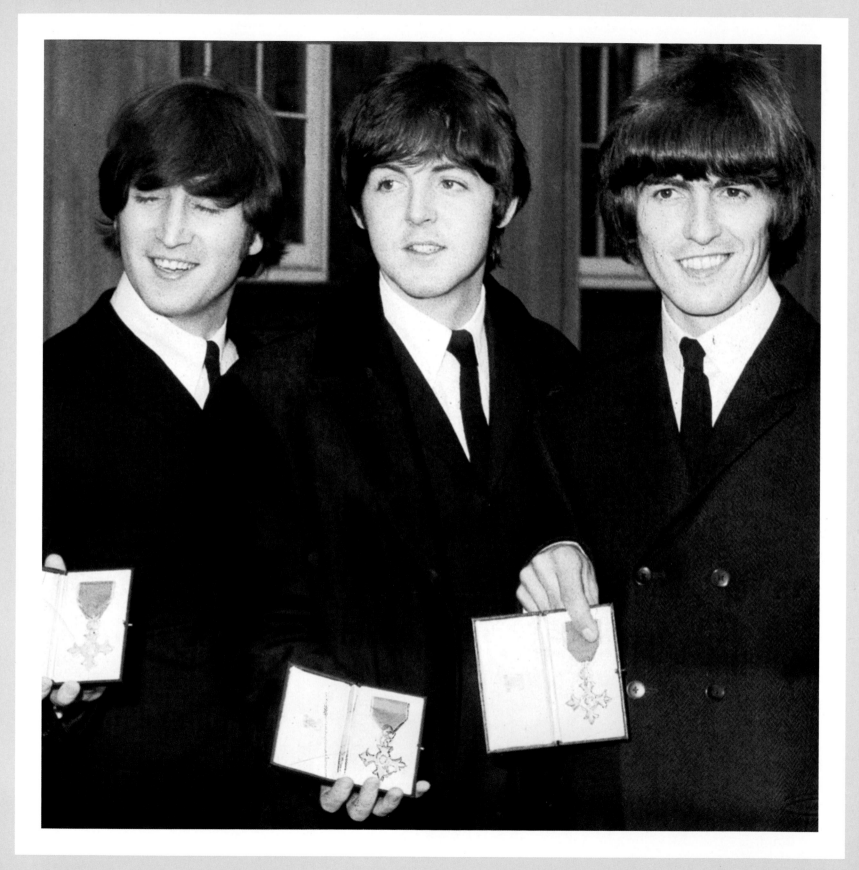

John Lennon, MBE

Opposite and above: While in the United States, John had finally met the hero that had inspired him to begin playing music as a teenager, "the King of Rock and Roll," Elvis Presley. However, the meeting turned out to be slightly uncomfortable for both parties, with John at first star-struck and then somewhat disillusioned, resulting in rather acerbic exchanges. However, having met "the King," it was not long before John and the boys found themselves in front of the Queen, receiving their MBEs. John initially had major reservations about accepting the award, wishing to distance himself from "the Establishment," but he relented, perhaps under pressure from Brian Epstein. At this time, the Beatles had begun work on the album *Rubber Soul*, which marked a period of transition as both the band and their music matured. John's writing became both more imaginative and introspective, as revealed by songs such as the Bob Dylan-influenced "Norwegian Wood" and the haunting "In My Life."

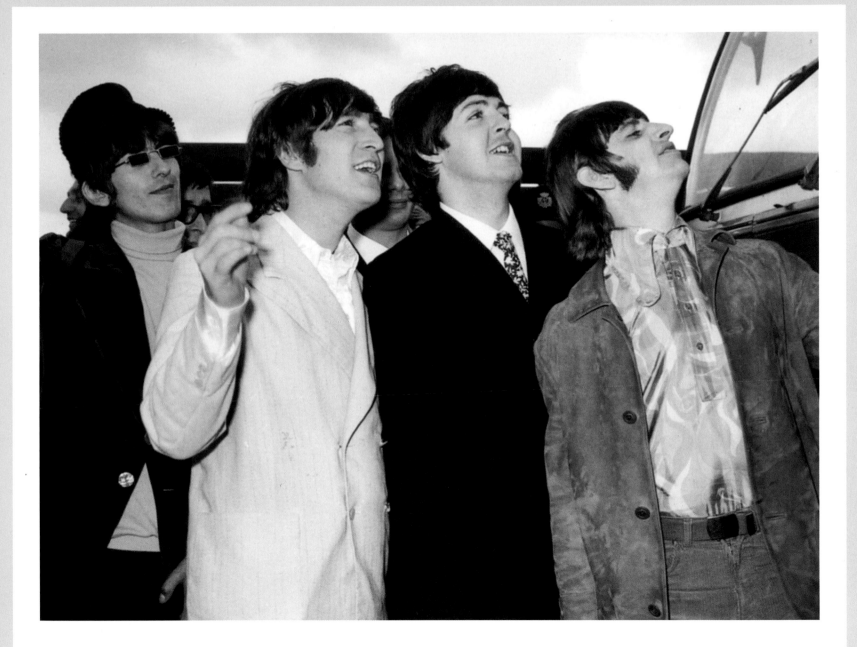

The music of Lennon and McCartney

Opposite: Happy to be surrounded by a bevy of beautiful showgirls, John and the boys filmed a television special, entitled *The Music of Lennon and McCartney*, at the beginning of November 1965. The show also featured Cilla Black, Lulu, and Marianne Faithfull. The program was broadcast in the run up to Christmas; this year there was no live Beatles Christmas show. Instead, the Beatles undertook a short British tour, which would prove to be their last.

Above: In the spring of 1966, the Beatles began work on their most ambitious album to date, *Revolver*. They had already broken the mold in writing almost all their own material and in jamming during studio time, now John would begin to realize his ambitions with regard to experimentation and studio-craft. Before the album was released the Beatles embarked on their final world tour, beginning in June with a return visit to Germany, where they had first cut their teeth as performers.

Disaster in Tokyo and Manila

Opposite: For some time, John had been longing to escape the madness of inaudible performances and focus on writing, but first there were obligations to fulfill. Just before setting off on their world tour, the Beatles performed a 15-minute set at the NME Annual Poll-Winners All-Star Concert at the Empire Pool, Wembley, on May 1, little knowing that it would be their last appearance at the event and, more remarkably, their last concert performance on British soil.

Above: As the world tour progressed, John became not just disillusioned, but increasingly frightened, and with good reason; when the Beatles arrived in Tokyo on June 29, they were told their lives had been threatened because they had been booked to perform at the sacred Budokan Hall. Things then worsened in Manila, in the Philippines, when the band failed to attend a meeting with the First Lady, Imelda Marcos.

August 1966: Death threats in America

Above and opposite: Safely back in Britain in July, John and the rest of the group attended a press conference, where they recounted their terrifying ordeal in the Philippines. Brian Epstein had apparently declined the invitation for the Beatles to meet with Imelda Marcos, thinking that that would be the end of the matter. However, the Philippine authorities took a somewhat different view, removing the group's police protection and making life difficult as the Beatles and their entourage attempted to flee the country, with some members of the party being physically assaulted. Just as the dust began to settle however, another row flared up that left John in fear for his safety. In March, he had given an interview to the London *Evening Standard* in which he had suggested that the Beatles were "more popular than Jesus," and now, on the eve of the U.S. leg of their tour, the interview was reprinted in an American teen magazine, provoking death threats and the burning of Beatles records and merchandise in the streets, and John was forced to explain himself to the press.

Apologizing to the press

Left: Before leaving for Chicago on August 11, John and the boys were taken on a relaxed tour around London Airport, including a visit to the new police facilities, before being waved off by the usual crowds of well-wishers. However, by the time they had reached their destination and checked into the Astor Towers hotel, and Brian Epstein had briefed John on the seriousness of the "more popular than Jesus" debacle that they were facing, John's anxiety levels were at an all-time high.

Opposite: As John prepared to apologize for his supposedly anti-Christian remarks at a televised press conference, he broke down in tears. Having composed himself, John made his "apology," although the more the assembled journalists pressed him for a simple "sorry," the more circuitous his explanation seemed to become. Nevertheless, it was enough to defuse the situation, at least for a time.

An end to touring

Opposite and above: Drained and perhaps rather dazed after the Chicago press conference, John had little time to collect his thoughts before the Beatles took to the stage, with dates in Chicago, Detroit, and Cleveland, followed by Washington, D.C., where members of the Ku Klux Klan staged a protest outside the stadium. Back in Britain, the eagerly awaited LP *Revolver* went straight into the album charts at number one, but in America even this wasn't enough to lift the mood in the Beatles camp. Klansmen were once again in attendance in Memphis, and when a firecracker exploded during the performance Paul and George were quick to check that John had not been shot. It was the final straw, and the boys decided that their touring days were over; their last date was at Candlestick Park, San Francisco, on August 29. They left America the following evening, and were only too happy to arrive safely back in Britain the next day.

How I Won The War

Left and opposite: Although John was almost certainly always the most independent of the Beatles, and had probably longed for an end to touring more than any of them—with the possible exception of George—now that the madness of life on the road had come to an end, he was faced with the problem of how to fill his time. He spent a few days immersed in domestic routine at Weybridge with Cynthia and Julian, but less than a week after returning from the North American tour, he was off again. This time he traveled to Hanover in West Germany, to begin work on his first solo movie role, as Private Gripweed in Dick Lester's anti-war satire *How I Won the War*. The part required an army regulation haircut for John, and also the donning of a pair of National Health Service spectacles, which soon became something of a trademark.

On location in Spain

Opposite and above: John had always been interested in the possibility of an acting career, and even as "Beatle John" he had often projected a larger-than-life persona both on and off stage, but whereas during the shooting of the Beatles' movies he had been required in front of the cameras for most of the scenes, this time his comparatively small part in *How I Won the War* made the filming process rather laborious. Filming lasted for around two months, with the shoot relocating to Almeria in southern Spain after Hamburg, where John enjoyed relaxing in the company of his co-stars Ronald Lacey and Michael Crawford. He was also visited by Cynthia, as well as Ringo and his wife, Maureen. However, equipped with a battered acoustic guitar and his trusty harmonica, John found time for some song writing during more solitary moments, in particular working on "Strawberry Fields Forever."

Strawberry Fields Forever

Left and opposite: John and Cynthia arrived back from Spain in early November 1966, after John had completed filming for *How I Won the War*. Although the experience had not been entirely satisfactory, and would in fact prove to be John's only film role without his fellow Beatles, the anti-war sentiment of the movie certainly appealed to him. At this time John was still yet to publicly denounce the war in Vietnam and to find fame as a peace campaigner, but he could soon be seen sporting the badge of the Campaign for Nuclear Disarmament. Toward the end of the month, guitar in hand, and armed with the bare bones of "Strawberry Fields Forever," John returned to the Abbey Road studios to be reunited for a recording session with his band-mates. The song, which combined nostalgic yearning with LSD-inspired, hallucinatory imagery, proved to be one of the Beatles' most complex recordings and, for many, one of their best.

Yoko Ono

Opposite: Just two days after he had returned from Spain, John and Cynthia were due to attend a party for the Who which Brian Epstein would be hosting at his apartment. However, at the last minute John decided that instead he would attend a preview of an exhibition at London's fashionable Indica Gallery, which was developing a reputation for hosting the work of some of the most avant-garde conceptual artists of the day. In this case, the exhibition was Yoko Ono's "Unfinished Paintings and Objects," and John found himself intrigued by both the work on display, and the artist herself, to whom he was introduced by gallery-owner John Dunbar.

Right: A still of John on location in London. At the end of November John made a return to the small screen, with his second appearance on Peter Cook and Dudley Moore's *Not Only ... But Also*, this time as a doorman at an exclusive club. The scene was actually shot outside a public lavatory in London.

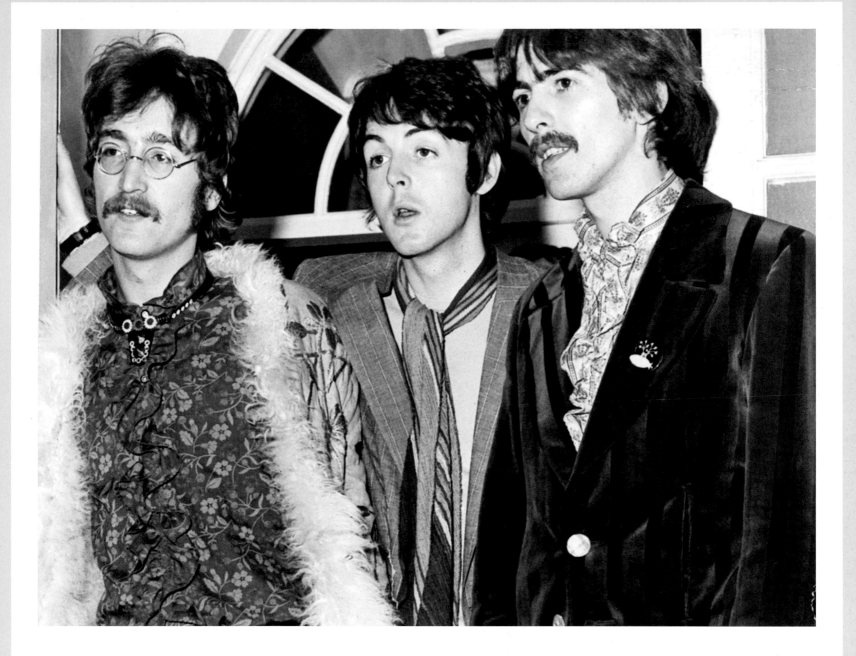

Sgt. Pepper's Lonely Hearts Club Band

Opposite and above: Freed from the pressures of touring and left with time on his hands, John spent much of the fall of 1966 watching television, smoking cannabis, and becoming increasingly distant from Cynthia, who failed to share his penchant for drugs. After returning to the recording studio, John found his creative appetite renewed—as did the rest of the band—although the next single, "Strawberry Fields Forever"/"Penny Lane", was the first in years not to top the charts.

However, the release of the *Sgt. Pepper's Lonely Hearts Club Band* LP in June 1967, heralded a revolution in the Beatles' approach to music, and also perhaps in popular music in general, and provided the perfect soundtrack for the "Summer of Love" in "Swinging London." The launch of the album was marked by a party and press conference at Brian Epstein's home.

Grammy-winning record sleeve

Right: As the album launch party revealed, not
only was the music of *Sgt. Pepper's* radical, but
so too was the packaging. The front of the
sleeve was graced with an iconic pop-art
collage by Peter Blake, and the back featured
the album's song lyrics, the first time lyrics
had been printed on a sleeve. The interior was
also novel, with a gatefold containing an
image of the Beatles in their day-glo military
attire, and a cardboard insert featuring cutout
medals and a mustache. In addition, early UK
releases also featured an abstract inner sleeve
produced by Dutch artists The Fool, who had
initially been considered to produce the front
cover design. The overall cost of producing the
sleeve is rumored to have been well over
£2000, probably making it the most expensive
ever made at that time. Brian Epstein was
seriously concerned that the overtly
psychedelic imagery would damage the
Beatles reputation, but the sleeve went on to
win a Grammy for Best Album Cover.

Part Two

Starting over

At home at Kenwood

Opposite: At times John could be content to spend time with Julian, read, watch television, or write music in his home studio. During the days of touring he often longed to be at home, but after spending so much time on the road he invariably found it difficult to adjust to domestic life upon his return, quickly becoming bored and restless. With touring over, John increasingly turned to LSD to fill the void, but while he could lose himself in psychedelic experiences, constant tripping did nothing to alleviate his insecurities.

Above: Kenwood, John and Cynthia's home in Weybridge, Surrey. Cynthia tried to provide as stable a home environment as possible for both her husband and son, turning a blind eye to John's frequent indiscretions and excesses. However, throughout 1967, John began to receive frequent postcards and even phone calls from Yoko Ono, putting his marriage under increasing strain.

All You Need is Love

Left and opposite: Two weeks after the release of the groundbreaking album *Sgt. Pepper's Lonely Hearts Club Band*, the Beatles began work on their contribution to the "Our World" broadcast, the first-ever global satellite link-up, involving 24 countries on five continents. As Britain's uncontested representatives of popular culture in 1967, the Beatles were selected to perform a song for the event. Both John and Paul came up with new offerings, but John's "All You Need Is Love" was selected as the most appropriate. The broadcast went out on June 25 to an estimated audience of 400 million viewers. The Beatles performed their vocals to the accompaniment of a live orchestra and a pre-recorded backing track. Joining them to sing the chorus were a number of celebrity friends, including Eric Clapton, Keith Moon, Marianne Faithfull, and members of the Rolling Stones. Released as a single a month later, John's simple song provided the band with a 12th UK number one record.

Buying an island

Opposite and right: In the summer of 1967 John hit upon the idea of establishing a private commune where the Beatles, their families, and other members of the band's inner circle, such as Brian Epstein, Neil Aspinall, and Mal Evans, could live in seclusion, away from the prying eyes of the press and public. It is thought that the idea was inspired by John's latest "guru," Alexis Mardas, or "Magic Alex," as John called him. Mardras, a young Greek man that John had met through the Indica Gallery, was full of surreal ideas and had a talent for electronics. At Mardas' suggestion, John decided to explore the possibility of purchasing a remote Greek island, and so on July 22, clad in "flower power" gear, and with "All You Need Is Love" topping the British charts, John, Cynthia, and Julian left for Greece with Paul and his girlfriend Jane Asher, in order to meet up with George, Pattie, Ringo, and Neil, who had arrived in Athens two days previously.

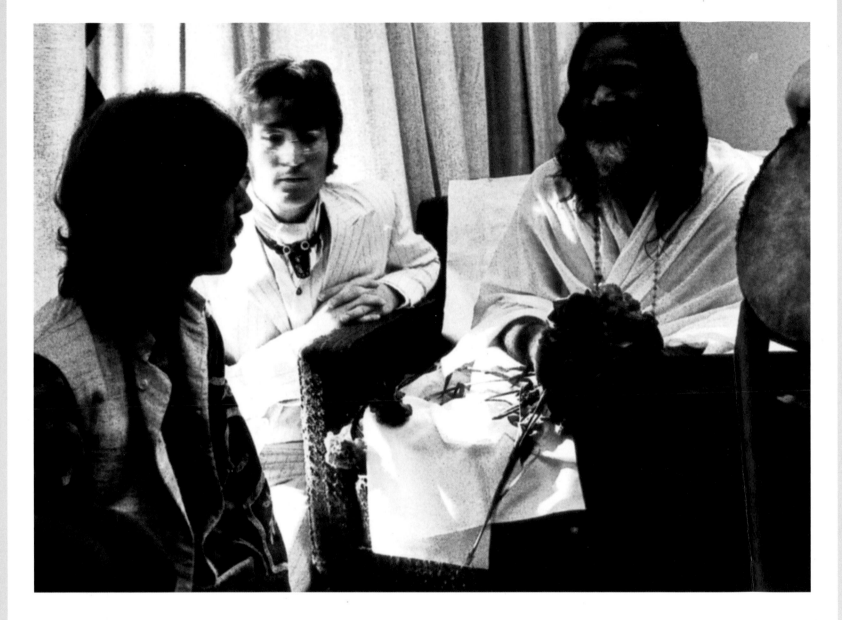

Enter the Maharishi

Opposite: John and Paul were the last to return from Greece at the end of the month, and as they flew into London Airport, rumors were rife that they had purchased an island in the Aegean. However, although they had entered into negotiations, any potential deal was scuppered by the distinct lack of privacy that they had encountered. Unknown to John and the rest of the scouting party, "Magic Alex" had been informing the authorities of the Beatles' movements at every step, so that the ruling Greek military junta might benefit from some positive public relations.

Above: With the idea of the Greek commune slipping away, John was still keen to find some sort of spiritual refuge, as were Paul and George, who were beginning to believe that LSD might not be the answer. In August 1967, George, who had already developed an interest in yoga and Eastern religions, took John and Paul to a lecture by the Maharishi Mahesh Yogi at the Hilton Hotel in London.

Following the Maharishi

Above and opposite: After the lecture the Beatles were invited to meet the Maharishi. Impressed by the Maharishi, John and the others decided to travel to Bangor in North Wales the following day, for a weekend retreat where they would learn more about the theory and practice of Transcendental Meditation. Accompanied by their partners, as well as Mick Jagger, Marianne Faithfull, and Donovan, the Beatles arrived at Euston Station to catch the train to Wales, but as they ran along the platform, Cynthia fell behind the others, and being mistaken for a fan, she was held back by a policeman. By the time John realized that she was missing the train had begun to move off, and Cynthia was forced to watch as it pulled out of the station with John calling from an open window. Cynthia arrived later by car, but the incident was a poignant symbol of the distance opening up between them. Brian Epstein was also due to make the journey to Bangor at the weekend, but tragically, on Sunday, August 27, he was found dead in his London apartment, having succumbed to a suspected accidental overdose.

Transcendental Meditation

Opposite and above: Shortly after Brian Epstein's death, John and George appeared on two editions of David Frost's new discussion show, *The Frost Programme*, where they talked about the relative virtues of LSD and Transcendental Meditation. The first program also featured an interview with the Maharishi Mahesh Yogi. John and the others were understandably devastated by Brian's death; although he had had less contact with the Beatles since their decision to stop touring, he had been there almost right from the start, and had been an important friend as well as helping them to reach the dizzying heights of fame. Outwardly though, John showed little emotion—it was not the first time that he had channeled his grief inwards. However, his newfound interest in Transcendental Meditation and Eastern philosophy undoubtedly helped him to cope, and he looked forward to traveling to India to continue his spiritual quest.

Magical Mystery Tour

Left and opposite: While John was uncertain about what effect Brian Epstein's death would have on the future of the Beatles, Paul was keen to press on with his *Magical Mystery Tour* project, which had stalled during the summer. At the beginning of September, plans to visit India were put on hold, and work on *The Magical Mystery Tour* began. Taking a cue from the LSD-fueled antics of Ken Kesey and the Merry Pranksters, who had traveled across California on a psychedelic voyage of discovery in 1965, the Beatles headed to the West Country for some largely improvised filming with an assortment of jobbing actors. The first night was spent in Teignmouth, Devon, before the coach headed south to Plymouth, having become stuck on a narrow bridge on the way to Widecombe. In Plymouth, John signed autographs for fans (left), and posed for the press photographers who had followed from London, before giving an interview for the local BBC news.

A clash of wills

Opposite and above: *The Magical Mystery Tour* experience did not prove to be an entirely happy one for John. He had traditionally had the final say in the Beatles' decision-making process, but now Paul was determined to exert executive control over the project, leading to frequent disagreements between the two of them, during both the location filming and the editing process. Afterwards, John expressed regret over the project, suggesting it was done simply to keep the fans happy. But most fans were sadly disappointed, believing—as did the majority of the critics—that the finished movie had suffered as a result of its haphazard production. Nevertheless, the soundtrack EP (which was given the full album treatment in the United States) contained some gems, with John being largely responsible for the surreal "I Am The Walrus," which proved to be one of the musical highlights of the piece.

Premiere of How I Won the War

Opposite and above: On October 18, the day after a memorial service was held in London in honor of Brian Epstein, John attended the London Pavilion for the world premiere of Dick Lester's *How I Won The War*, which he had filmed a year earlier. All of the Beatles were in attendance with their respective partners, but although John arrived with Cynthia on his arm, a mutual infatuation had been developing between him and Yoko Ono. Just days before, Yoko's latest exhibition

"Yoko Plus Me", had opened at the Lisson Gallery, with John's financial support. Cynthia could not fail to be aware of Yoko's existence, for the artist had bombarded John with a steady stream of letters and phone calls since they met, and on more than one occasion Yoko had turned up unannounced at their home. However, having confronted John about the matter, Cynthia seemed not to perceive this curious Japanese woman as a threat.

Launch of Apple

Opposite and above: On December 5, 1967, John, Cynthia and the Harrisons attended the launch party of the Apple Boutique. The store in Baker Street sold clothing and accessories, selected or designed by the art collective called The Fool. With *The Magical Mystery Tour* largely complete, each of the Beatles began to focus on solo projects, although at the same time collective plans were being put in place for the launch of a new company. Apple Music Ltd. had already replaced Beatles Ltd. in May, essentially to exploit a tax loophole, but more ambitious and supposedly altruistic schemes were afoot, beginning with the launch of Apple Retail, and then the opening of the Apple Boutique.

Beatlemania in miniature

Opposite and above: John had intended that the launch party for the Apple Boutique to be "by invitation only," but numerous gatecrashers made their way in, with the crowds surging forward as John and George arrived. To John the scene was something like "Beatlemania" in miniature, which rather put a dampener on the proceedings. Once open, however, the outlet received less custom than expected, although shoplifting became rife.

In 1965, John and George had founded Haylings Supermarkets Ltd., which they had turned over to John's school-friend Pete Shotton, a former member of the Quarry Men, and it was he who was brought in to run the boutique. However, the combination of shoplifting and the expensive tastes of The Fool meant the project was hemorrhaging money from the outset, and the shop closed less than a year after opening. On July 30, 1968 the remaining stock was freely distributed to the public, again triggering chaotic scenes.

Party time

Right: The UK release of the six-track *Magical Mystery Tour* EP, which fell on the day after the opening of the Apple Boutique, was celebrated with a launch party at the Lancaster Hotel, London. John arrived in fancy dress. In the run-up to Christmas, there were other functions to attend, including a party for fan-club secretaries in Mayfair. Meanwhile, *The Magical Mystery Tour* narrowly missed the top of the charts, stalling at number two, while the movie, screened in black and white on December 26 and in color on January 5, received a mauling by the press.

Opposite: John with Cynthia, "Magic Alex," and George. At around this time, John was visited by his father, Alfred Lennon, who was seeking his son's blessing—and financial support—in order to marry his 19-year-old fiancée, Pauline Jones. It had been three years since Fred had reappeared in John's life for the first time since childhood, and contact had been intermittent ever since, but nevertheless John agreed to help.

Apple go to the Big Apple

Left and opposite: John and Paul traveling to New York in April 1968. In January, John had returned to the studio with the Beatles to make some new recordings, before they headed off to Rishikesh in India in February. The intention was to spend three months studying Transcendental Meditation with the Maharishi Mahesh Yogi, accompanied by their partners, and in the company of such spiritual converts as Donovan, the Beach Boys' Mike Love, and Mia Farrow. However, the sojourn was cut short in early April after "Magic Alex" arrived and intimated that the Maharishi was seducing his female students, prompting John to write the scathing "Sexy Sadie." Within days of his return, John's thoughts had turned away from meditation and asceticism, and back toward business and the launch of Apple Corps and its numerous possible subsidiaries. So in early May John and Paul headed to the United States to announce the formation of their umbrella organization, and to discuss their business ideas.

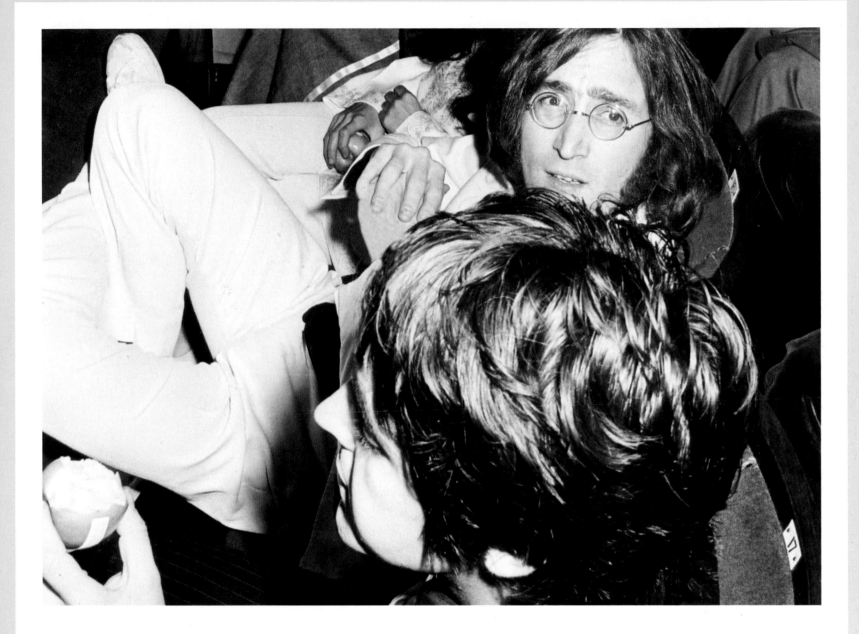

Yoko goes public

Opposite: John and Yoko at the premiere of the stage adaptation of John's book *In His Own Write*. Unbeknown to Cynthia, while she and John were in India he had been receiving regular correspondence from Yoko Ono. Upon his return from the United States, having persuaded his wife to take a vacation in Greece with "Magic Alex" and Pattie Harrison's sister Jenny, John invited Yoko to Kenwood, where they spent the night recording before making love in the morning. When Cynthia returned a couple of days later, she found them together and left to stay with Jenny. That night, John and Yoko made their first public appearance together at the launch of Apple Tailoring, but it was at the June premiere of *In His Own Write*, which had been adapted for the stage with the help of Victor Spinetti, that the press finally took notice. By the time of the premiere of the Beatles' animated feature, *Yellow Submarine*, a month later (above), John and Cynthia had separated, and he and Yoko were rarely apart.

You Are Here

Opposite and right: On July 1, 1968, both dressed in white, John and Yoko attended the opening of John's first art exhibition, entitled "You Are Here," which he had dedicated to Yoko and which was marked by the release of 365 helium-filled balloons. John also publicly declared his love for Yoko at the exhibition, despite the fact that they were both still married to other people. In Yoko, John was convinced that he had found "the one", the intellectual and creative equal who had awoken him from his creative slumbers— but also someone he could completely relax with, remarking that he could happily take her to the pub like an old friend from Liverpool. Yoko also undoubtedly represented an escape for John: from his marriage; from Kenwood; perhaps, he hoped, even from fame, money, and the Beatles. However, by now they were both regularly using heroin.

Busted!

Above and opposite: In October John and Yoko, who were now living at Ringo's Montagu Square flat, were arrested for obstruction and the possession of cannabis. John had apparently been tipped off about the raid, but the Beatles, it seemed, were no longer untouchable. However, despite the emotional turmoil that John had been experiencing due to the break-up of his marriage, or perhaps because of it, he had been enjoying a particularly prolific period of songwriting. By the time the Beatles reconvened in the summer of 1968, he had come up with around 11 songs to take into the studio, many of them first developed in India. Paul and George had also been writing individually, but the new sessions would begin with John's "Revolution." John was accompanied into the studio by Yoko, who became an almost permanent fixture at all future sessions, much to the chagrin of his band mates.

Charged with possession

Above: Having been charged with possession of drugs, John and Yoko appeared at Marylebone Magistrates' Court on October 19, where they were bailed to return the following month. Both of them knew that a drugs conviction could make life difficult, particularly if they wished to visit the United States. Just days later, Yoko announced that she was pregnant with John's child, but she miscarried soon afterwards. When the verdict was announced, John was fined for possession and charges against Yoko were dropped.

Opposite: In early December, John, Yoko, and Julian joined Brian Jones and the rest of the Rolling Stones as guests on the Stones' planned television special, *The Rolling Stones Rock and Roll Circus*. The end of 1968 was an important period for John; he and Cynthia were divorced in early November, just prior to the release of John and Yoko's LP, *Unfinished Music No. 1: Two Virgins*, with its controversial cover depicting John and Yoko naked. At the end of the month, the Beatles' eponymous double album, which became better known as the *White Album*, was also released.

Solo Beatle

Opposite: John was not only invited to the filming of *The Rolling Stones Rock and Roll Circus* as an audience member, but also as an active participant. He performed "Yer Blues," with a backing group, The Dirty Mac, consisting of Keith Richards, Eric Clapton, and Mitch Mitchell. As if to highlight the fractured state of the Beatles at this time, it was the first occasion that John had performed publicly without the rest of the group, but despite this Paul was pressing for the band to return to live performance as soon as possible.

Right: On the same day that rehearsals began for the Rolling Stones' project, John and Cynthia's former home, Kenwood, in Weybridge, Surrey, was put up for sale. Cynthia soon became romantically involved with Roberto Bassanini, the owner of the Italian hotel to which she had retreated in June, following her separation from John. Cynthia and Roberto married, on August 1, 1970.

In the studio

Left and opposite: Recording the *White Album* had been a struggle for all involved, with each of the Beatles working in separate studios at times. Nevertheless, John had been pleased with the development and direction of his songwriting, even if his band mates had been exasperated by his drug use and Yoko's constant presence—not to mention her criticism. As 1969 began, Paul continued to hope that the Beatles might perform live once more, but the idea was soon shelved in favor of a return to the studio, which was documented on film, and gave rise to the Beatles final album release, *Let it Be*. Early in the proceedings, which were initially known as the "Get Back" sessions, George quit the band after arguing with both John and Paul, but although John remarked that he could be replaced by Eric Clapton, he was persuaded back. Meanwhile, American organist Billy Preston was drafted in for the sessions, partly in the hope that his presence would ease tension in the studio. However, in the background, financial disputes were brewing, as John, George, and Ringo allied themselves with American lawyer Allen Klein.

Playing to the rooftops

Opposite: With the "Get Back" sessions drawing to a close at the end of January, the Beatles decided to emerge from the makeshift studio installed in the basement of the Apple building and take to the rooftop, where they delivered their last-ever performance together. With John in fine voice, and clad in a fur coat, the band played for just over 40 minutes, bringing the street below to a standstill until the police politely asked them to stop. John famously ended the set with the ironic remark, "...I hope we passed the audition."

Above: A few days later Yoko obtained a divorce from her husband, Tony Cox, and on March 20, John and Yoko were married at the British Consulate in Gibraltar. From there they traveled to Paris, where they dined with the surrealist painter Salvador Dali before heading to the Amsterdam Hilton on March 25, where they began a week-long "bed-in" in the name of world peace.

John speaks out

Above: Although John had always been independent, freethinking, and outspoken, he had tended to suppress his more controversial or outlandish views—largely at the request of Brian Epstein, who had wished to present a carefully manicured image of his boys to the world's press. However, with Epstein's passing, and emboldened by Yoko, John no longer tried to bite his tongue or to suppress his avant-garde leanings. Some members of the press and public, and even close friends, began to wonder if he was simply courting attention, or had perhaps begun to lose his mind.

Opposite: On March 31, John and Yoko left Amsterdam to travel to Vienna for the premiere of their film *Rape*, which satirized media intrusion. The film was followed by a press conference at the Hotel Sacher, which John and Yoko delivered from within a large sack.

Plant an acorn for peace

Left and opposite: The following day John and Yoko arrived in London, where they attended a press conference, stating that they intended to send a pair of acorns to every world leader, thus encouraging them to plant trees rather than drop bombs. Interestingly, the previous June, John and Yoko had each planted an acorn outside Coventry Cathedral as part of a National Sculpture Exhibition. Following the press conference, John and Yoko made a live appearance on the *Today* program for Thames Television, which was hosted by Eamonn Andrews. As in Vienna, they were interviewed inside a large, white sack, and once again promoted the idea of world peace and their concept of "bagism." However on this occasion, perhaps because it was April Fool's Day, they managed to persuade the interviewer to join them in their bag.

At home with the Lennons

Above: Yoko in the kitchen of Tittenhurst Park, a vast Georgian mansion with a 60-acre park that John purchased in May 1969 for the two of them to live in. Although John was still in contact with his bandmates, and notably recorded "The Ballad of John and Yoko" with Paul in April, he was becoming increasingly focused on his relationship and projects with Yoko.

Opposite: On April 21, the Lennons established their book and music publishing company Bag Productions, and the following day, John officially changed his middle name, "Winston," to "Ono," with the ceremony being conducted on the roof of the Apple building. As May began, John and Yoko released their second experimental LP, *Unfinished Music 2: Life With The Lions*, before being joined by Yoko's daughter, Kyoko, who had arrived from New York.

Give Peace A Chance

Opposite: Amid mounting financial and legal concerns, centering around Apple Corps, John and Yoko spent some time in London with Kyoko, before heading for the Bahamas. They had hoped to travel to the United States, but John had been denied a visa due to his conviction for cannabis possession. From the Bahamas, John and Yoko headed for Montreal, Canada, to stage their second week-long "bed-in," during which time the anthemic "Give Peace A Chance" was recorded.

Above: In July, "Give Peace A Chance," which was attributed to the Plastic Ono Band, became the first solo single released by a Beatle. Attempting to put their differences aside, the Beatles returned to the studio in the summer of 1969 to begin work on a new album, and at the end of the sessions in September, John, George, and Ringo attended the Isle of Wight Festival to watch Bob Dylan.

Planning for the future

Opposite and above: After returning from Canada in July, John and Yoko visited John's cousin Stanley in Edinburgh, accompanied by Kyoko and Julian. However, while driving to the Highlands, John crashed his Austin Maxi into a ditch, and both he and Yoko sustained facial injuries. A few days later John was well enough to join the Beatles in the studio for the sessions that would result in the album *Abbey Road*, but, like the "Get Back" sessions, these were strained, with proceedings frequently descending into argument.

With the sessions largely complete, John and Yoko continued to focus on their projects together, holding an evening of their films at the Institute of Contemporary Art on September 10, before returning to Canada for the live debut of the Plastic Ono Band on September 13, alongside Eric Clapton, Klaus Voormann, and Alan White. It was apparently while flying to Toronto that John decided that he would leave the Beatles.

Returning the MBE

Above and opposite: In October, with *Abbey Road* at the top of the UK album charts and the single "Something"/"Come Together" in the top five, John and Yoko released "Cold Turkey," backed with "Don't Worry Kyoko (Mummy's Only Looking For Her hand In The Snow)," which was credited to the Plastic Ono Band. John and Yoko's third experimental LP, *The Wedding Album*, followed in early November. Continuing his efforts to campaign for world peace, on October 25 John returned his MBE to Buckingham Palace, sending an offhand letter to both the Queen and the Prime Minister, Harold Wilson citing as the reasons for his decision the government's position on the wars in Vietnam and Nigeria, and the relatively poor performance of his latest single. Just as he had hoped, the decision sparked huge controversy and media interest, and John was to spend the day fielding calls from the press, as well as his disgruntled Aunt Mimi.

Campaign for Hanratty

Opposite and above: In early December, John was nominated by anthropologist Desmond Morris as his "Man of the Decade," following which, the BBC spent several days filming the Lennons for a documentary entitled "The World of John and Yoko." On December 10, John and Yoko met with the parents of James Hanratty, who had been hanged for the murder of a scientist in 1962. There had long been doubts over the safety of Hanratty's conviction, and the Lennons announced plans to make a film about the case, which they hoped would establish his innocence. The government had suspended capital punishment for five years in 1965—partly due to the outcry over the Hanratty case—and with a review of the suspension imminent, John and Yoko decided to lend their weight to the campaign for the abolition of the death penalty. The day after meeting the Hanrattys, John and Yoko could be found protesting outside the Kensington Odeon, where Ringo's *The Magic Christian* was receiving its royal world charity premiere.

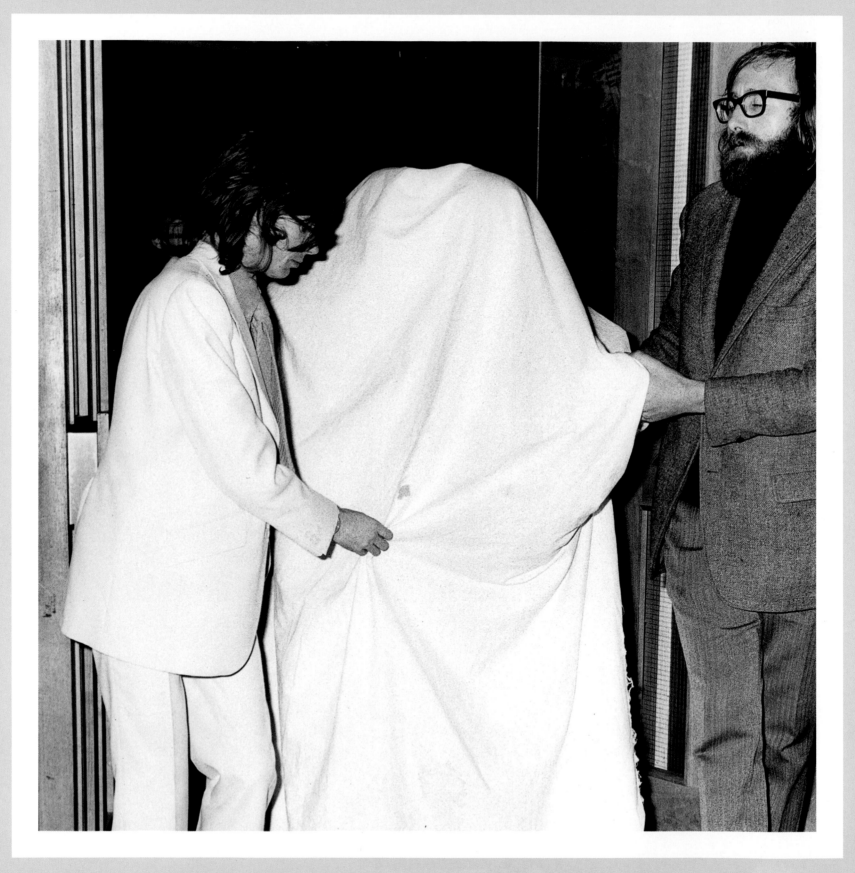

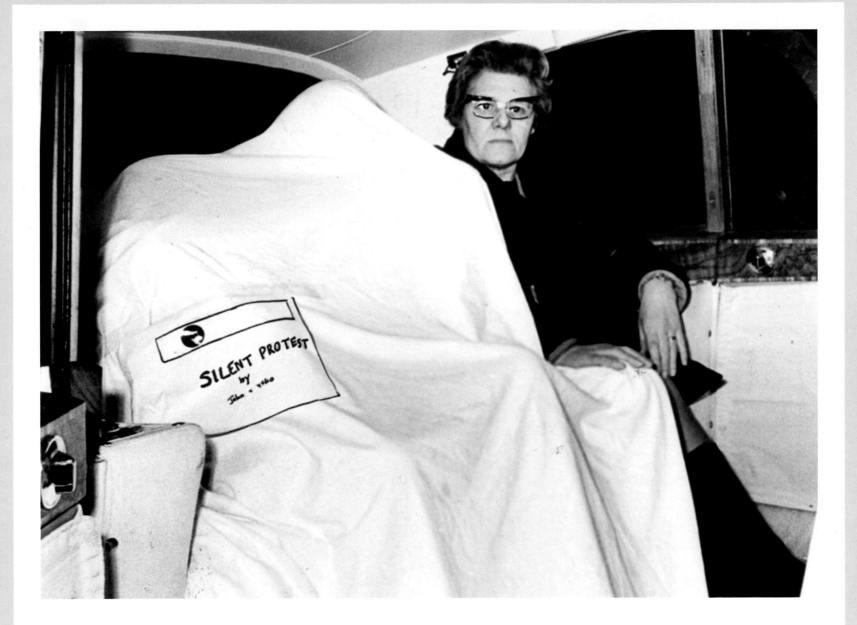

Bagism for protest

Opposite and above: A few days after their Kensington protest, John and Yoko accompanied James Hanratty's parents to Speakers Corner, Hyde Park, where Hanratty's father made a speech proclaiming his son's innocence. Traveling in John's white Rolls-Royce, John and Yoko arrived inside a large white sack bearing the legend "Silent Protest by John and Yoko," and "Britain Murdered Hanratty." Afterwards, a petition calling for an end to capital punishment was taken to Downing Street.

John and Yoko's "bagism" concept was based primarily on the idea that you could not be judged for your appearance if you were concealed within a sack but, as in this case, it could also be used as an intriguing vehicle for non-verbal and non-violent protest. During the Montreal "bed-in," John had urged non-violence on the students protesting at Berkley; and in November, "Give Peace A Chance" had been adopted as the song of choice by some 250,000 anti-Vietnam protesters who had marched on the White House.

The Plastic Ono Band

Above and opposite: On December 12, the Plastic Ono Band issued the album "Live Peace In Toronto," and just three days later, they returned to the stage for another impromptu performance, this time with a line-up that included George, Billy Preston, Eric Clapton, and Keith Moon in addition to John and Yoko. The concert, which was entitled "Peace For Christmas," was held in aid of the charity UNICEF at London's Lyceum Ballroom, and provided the Lennons with the opportunity to deliver their message, "War Is Over."

By this time, John had told the Beatles that he was leaving the group, although he had been persuaded not to announce his decision publicly, at least for the time being. There were still numerous legal and financial matters that would need resolution before the band could be officially dissolved, even if they had decided to put a permanent stop to recording. However, privately Paul hoped that, given time, John would change his mind.

The World of John and Yoko

Opposite: On the same day that the Plastic Ono Band made its London concert debut at the Lyceum, the BBC screened the recently-filmed documentary, "The World of John and Yoko." The following day the Lennons returned to Toronto, where John announced his plans to organize a peace festival. While in Canada, he also conveyed his message of peace to the Canadian Prime Minister, Pierre Trudeau.

Right: From Canada, John and Yoko headed to Denmark, where they spent a month vacationing with Yoko's daughter, Kyoko, her father Tony Cox, and his wife, Melinda. While they were away, on January 15, an exhibition of John's lithographs, entitled "Bag One," opened at the London Arts Gallery. However, the following day, police raided the exhibition, confiscating eight artworks and closing it down on the grounds of obscenity. Nevertheless, the remaining works were shipped to the United States just days later, to be exhibited in Detroit.

War is Over

Left: Over the Christmas period, John and Yoko re-affirmed their peace message by hiring billboards in 11 cities across the world, and distributing thousands of posters which bore the message "War Is Over! If You Want It. Happy Christmas from John and Yoko," words which would later form the basis of John's song "Happy Christmas (War Is Over)."

Opposite: Earlier in the year, John had caused some offence with the return of his MBE and the suggestion that he was becoming ashamed of his country, and many people had long felt distanced by his increasingly eccentric behavior. However, while the *Daily Mirror* labeled John as 1969's "Clown of the Year," readers of *Disc and Music Echo* voted him as their favorite Beatle, with many also expressing their support for John and Yoko's peace campaigning.

Cropped tops

Above and opposite: Returning from Denmark in late January 1970, where they had both had their hair cropped, John and Yoko went into the studio to record John's latest song, "Instant Karma," with George, Billy Preston, and Eric Clapton once again joining them as the Plastic Ono Band. However, this time, Phil Spector produced the session. Controversially, Spector soon also began remixing the "Get Back" sessions to produce the Beatles' final album release, *Let It Be*, which outraged both Paul and George Martin. A few days after recording "Instant Karma" the Lennons visited civil rights campaigner and leader of the UK "Black Power" movement Michael X at his Holloway headquarters. Here they exchanged their shorn locks for a pair of Muhammad Ali's boxing trunks, both of which would later be auctioned to raise money for charity. Michael X also joined John and Yoko for an appearance on LWT's *The Simon Dee Show*.

Primal scream

Opposite and above : Although John and Yoko still appeared to be very much in love, by early 1970 John had once again become withdrawn— no doubt due to his continued battles with addiction, Paul, and the disintegration of the Beatles. As a result, he decided to begin "Primal Scream" therapy, based on the teachings of Dr. Arthur Janov, who became directly involved in his treatment. Janov's methods involved attempting to literally scream away emotional pain, which in John's case seemed to stem largely from the loss of his mother, and his father's absence during childhood. In late April, John visited the United States for further treatment with Janov. However, as the month began, it was Paul that was struggling to contain his anger that Phil Spector had completed the production on the *Let It Be* album, authorized by John, George, and Ringo. Paul was incensed, and further embittered, when his bandmates attempted to delay the release of his first solo album, *McCartney*, to avoid a clash with *Let It Be*. On April 10, 1970, Paul had released a statement announcing that he had left the Beatles.

New projects

Opposite and above: In the spring and summer of 1970 John spent a number of weeks in the United States receiving therapy at Dr. Janov's Los Angeles treatment center, during which time he announced his intention to settle in New York. While there he also began to write a number of new, emotionally charged songs, and he spent the fall back in England recording his first real solo album, *John Lennon/Plastic Ono Band*. Shortly after the release of the album in December, John and Yoko began work on two new films, entitled *Up Your Legs Forever* and *Fly*. In the spring of 1971 the Lennons appeared on the chat show *Parkinson*, when they discussed, among other things, the demise of the Beatles—refuting Yoko's supposed involvement in the break-up of the band—and their commitment to avant-garde art, which, they explained, was better understood in the United States. The following month, however, John and Yoko flew to Cannes, where *Fly* and another of their films, *Apotheosis (Balloon)*, received their premieres.

Cannes Film Festival

Opposite and above: Stopping in Nice on their way to the Cannes Film Festival, John and Yoko appeared relaxed. However, John was disappointed with the reaction to his film *Apotheosis (Balloon)*, which simply followed the course of a helium balloon as it rose into the sky and disappeared among the clouds. Both he and Yoko were very passionate about their art and its worthiness, but they were often frustrated by a public that seemed to constantly doubt the sincerity of their intentions.

During the summer, with John having been granted a nine-month United States visa, the Lennons began their battle for custody of Yoko's daughter Kyoko. They also had time for more leisurely pursuits, and John was pleased to find he could walk around New York relatively freely. While in North America, the couple also appeared on stage with Frank Zappa at the Fillmore East, and John began work on his next album, *Imagine*, which he completed at his home studio at Tittenhurst Park.

A working class hero

Left: John's recent musical output had become far less whimsical, and prior to the release of *Imagine*, which he would later describe as "sugar-coated," John could be found promoting two of his most politically charged singles, "Power To The People," and "Working Class Hero." These songs appeared to reflect both John's deepening involvement in political affairs and the soul-searching inspired by his primal therapy, with "Power To The People" a sloganeering call to action, and "Working Class Hero" an embittered rant at society.

Opposite: Around the same time that John was putting the finishing touches to his *Imagine* album, Yoko re-released her book *Grapefruit*, which had previously been issued on a limited edition basis. The book, which had so intrigued John after he and Yoko had met, contained numerous short compositions, which—despite appearing to take the form of poetry— were essentially concepts, or directions, many of which Yoko and John would realize in their art projects.

Living in New York

Opposite: John performing at a charity concert in New York. On September 3, shortly before the release of *Imagine*, John and Yoko flew to New York where they took up residence at the St. Regis Hotel, before settling in an apartment in November. By this time, *Imagine* had topped the charts on both sides of the Atlantic, Yoko had returned to the New York avant-garde art scene with a one-woman show, and both of them had begun to associate with a number of left-wing political activists. In 1972, even before the release of the explicitly political "Some Time In New York City," the authorities instigated proceedings to have John

deported. John never again returned to Britain, fighting his case on the grounds that his UK drugs conviction was unsafe, that he was being harassed by government agents, and that he needed to be in the United States due to the custody battle for Kyoko. John and Yoko had traveled to North America seeking sanctuary, but by the fall of 1973 both were feeling hounded and worn-out, and they decided to separate, with John leaving New York for California, escorted by their secretary, May Pang (above, with John).

Lost weekend

Above and opposite: Separated from Yoko, John indulged in an extended period of drinking and partying, during which time he became romantically involved with May Pang (above). However, the separation turned into a 15-month-long "lost weekend," with John effectively in exile. Depressed and restless, his bouts of drunkenness did nothing to lighten his mood, and although he began work on a rock 'n' roll album with Phil Spector, the sessions quickly descended into chaos. However, by September 1974, John had straightened himself out and,

almost a year after the release of his *Mind Games* LP, he issued *Walls and Bridges*. The album topped the American charts, as did the single "Whatever Gets You Through The Night," which featured backing vocals by Elton John. John returned the favor by joining Elton on stage at Madison Square Garden in November, which would prove to be Lennon's last concert appearance. Shortly afterwards, John also collaborated with David Bowie (opposite), appearing on his version of "Across The Universe" and co-writing and recording "Fame."

Back to New York ... and Yoko

Above: John pictured with Mick Jagger during the days of his "lost weekend." In early January 1975, John returned to live with Yoko at the Dakota building in New York. Just days later, the Beatles & Co. was officially dissolved by the High Court in London.

Opposite: Having rescued his tapes from Phil Spector, John released his *Rock 'n' Roll* album in February 1975, and the following month appeared as a guest presenter at the Grammy Awards. It was his first public engagement and his first appearance with Yoko, who was once

again pregnant, since their reunion. In September John was still contesting the deportation order, but a temporary halt was granted on the grounds of Yoko's pregnancy. Three weeks later, John finally received the news he had been waiting for: on October 7 the deportation order was overturned. Two days afterward there was further cause for celebration: it was John's 35th birthday, and Yoko gave birth to their son, Sean Taro Ono Lennon. In November, John released the album *Shaved Fish*, before announcing his retirement from music to spend time with his family.

Death of a Beatle

It would be some five years before John
returned to recording, entering the studio
with Yoko in August 1980 to start work on
their *Double Fantasy* LP, which was released
by Geffen Records in November. This was
preceded by an extensive interview with
Playboy magazine and the release of the
single "(Just Like) Starting Over." As
December began John and Yoko were still
visiting the recording studios almost every
day and, as he explained to his Aunt Mimi
on December 6, he hoped to return to
Britain soon, with plans to embark on a
world tour. John also gave an interview to
BBC Radio's Andy Peebles that day. On
December 8 John and Yoko were
photographed for the cover of *Rolling Stone*
magazine by Annie Leibovitz. Later that
evening, John and Yoko left the Dakota
building for the Record Plant studios, with
John pausing to sign an autograph for Mark
Chapman, who was still waiting outside
when John and Yoko returned shortly before
11 p.m. Calling out "Mr Lennon?", Chapman
fired five bullets into John's back and arm,
and although he was rushed to hospital, his
injuries would prove fatal.

"... Please pray the same for him..."

Opposite and above: By the morning, tributes to John filled the newspapers and the airwaves, and a huge crowd had gathered at the Dakota Building, with similar scenes repeated around the world, as fans congregated to share their grief. Ringo and Barbara Bach flew from the Bahamas and Julian Lennon came from England to be Yoko and five-year-old Sean. On December 9 Yoko issued a statement saying "There is no funeral for John. John loved and prayed for the human race. Please pray the same for him. Love, Yoko and Sean." John was cremated at Ferncliff Mortuary, Hartsdale, New York, on December 10. Later Mark Chapman was found guilty of murder and was sent to in Attica Correctional Facility, where he remains today.

An outpouring of grief

Opposite and above: In St. George's Square, Liverpool, thousands of grief-stricken fans assembled for a memorial service and candlelit vigil, and on December 14 a day of mourning was held in several cities, with many thousands of fans assembling in Liverpool and New York to observe ten minutes silence at Yoko's request, beginning at 7 p.m. GMT (2 p.m. EST). It was ironic, and unthinkable, that a man who had dedicated himself to preaching peace and love had been so senselessly murdered. For the rest of the year and beyond, John's music was almost inescapable, with the airwaves reverberating to the sounds of "Imagine" and "Give Peace A Chance", and numerous television and radio programs dedicated to discussions of the man and his music. Meanwhile, the album *Double Fantasy* and the single "(Just Like) Starting Over" topped the charts on both sides of the Atlantic.

Conspiracy theories

Opposite and above: It was not long until conspiracy theories began to surface, suggesting that John was not simply murdered by an unhinged individual, but was subject to a political assassination, possibly by agents of the US government. It later emerged that the authorities had kept a watchful eye on John since his arrival in America because of his anti-Vietnam protests and associations with other political activists, but claims that the FBI or CIA were directly involved in his death have remained unsubstantiated. Within weeks of John's death, *Double*

Fantasy had sold over a million copies, and the single "Woman" provided another posthumous UK number one. In May 1981, George Harrison released his tribute to John, "All Those Years Ago". At the end of the year, fans gathered outside the Cavern Club in Liverpool, to mark the first anniversary of John Lennon's death and an annual memorial service was inaugurated outside Capitol Records in Hollywood.

Starting over

Opposite: In 1986, Yoko arrived in London with Sean to embark upon the "Star of Peace" tour. Since 1970, Yoko Ono had suffered a great deal at the hands of the press, particularly in Britain, where she had been vilified for supposedly bringing about the Beatles' demise. However, in the wake of John's death, she was treated somewhat more favorably; being afforded a measure of respect for her dignity. In February 1982, Yoko and Sean collected the Best Album Grammy for *Double Fantasy*, and two years later, Yoko opened Strawberry Fields, a memorial dedicated to John in Central Park, New York. 1984 would also see the release of *Milk and Honey*, the final LP credited to John Lennon and Yoko Ono. In addition to performing, Yoko has continued to campaign for various charitable causes, including the Spirit Foundation, which she had established with John.

Left: Julian Lennon pictured in 1983. Shortly after the death of his father, Julian embarked on a musical career and in 1985 was nominated for a Grammy as Best New Artist. At the beginning of the 1990s he took a break from music, returning in 1998 with the album *Photograph Smile*.

Chronology

1940

Oct 9 John Winston Lennon is born to Julia and Alfred Lennon at the Oxford Street Maternity Hospital, Liverpool. Alfred is absent.

1941

John is primarily cared for by his aunt and uncle, Mary (Aunt Mimi) and George, at 251 Menlove Avenue, Woolton.

1942

Apr John's father leaves home, having been away at sea for much of the time since his son's birth.

1945

Sept John attends school at Dovedale Primary, Liverpool.

1957

March John forms The Blackjacks skiffle group, soon to be renamed The Quarry Men.

24 May The Quarry Men make their debut public performance at a street carnival, Roseberry Street, Liverpool.

6 Jul John meets Paul McCartney for the first time, when The Quarry Men play at St Peter's church summer fete.

20 Jul Paul joins The Quarry Men.

7 Aug The Quarry Men perform their debut at Liverpool's Cavern Club.

Sept John enrols at Liverpool College of Art

1958

6 Feb George Harrison joins The Quarry Men, having watched them perform at Wilson Hall, Liverpool.

15 Jul John's mother Julia is killed by a car whilst crossing the road outside Aunt Mimi's house.

1960

10 May The Quarry Men become The Beatals.

2 Jun They perform at Neston Institute as The Beatles.

Jul John leaves art college.

August The Beatles secure a stint in Hamburg where they meet Ringo Starr.

1961

9 Feb The group play their first Cavern Club gig as The Beatles.

Dec Brian Epstein offers to manage The Beatles, John accepts on their behalf.

9 May Brian Epstein secures a contract for The Beatles with Parlophone, a subsidiary of EMI.

4 Jun Brian and the Beatles are signed to EMI, recording their first session at Abbey Road studios two days later.

15 Aug Ringo Starr, joins the Beatles

23 Aug John marries Cynthia Powell at Mount Pleasant Register Office, Liverpool. Cynthia is pregnant.

5 Oct "Love Me Do," backed with "P.S. I Love You" is released as the Beatles first single.

1963

22 Mar The album *Please Please Me* is released.

8 Apr John becomes a father as Cynthia gives birth to a son, John Charles Julian Lennon.

3 Aug The Beatles perform for the last time at the Cavern Club.

22 Nov UK release of *With the Beatles*

1964

2 Mar The Beatles begin shooting their first film, *A Hard Day's Night*.

23 Mar *In His Own Write*, John's first book, is published.

26 Jun The album *A Hard Day's Night* is released in the US (July 10 in the UK)

6 Jul The Beatles' film *A Hard Day's Night* premieres in London.

18 Aug The Beatles leave London for their first major US tour.

1965

24 Jun John's second book, *A Spaniard In The Works* is published.

29 Jul The Beatles second movie *Help!*, premieres in London.

8 Aug Release of the album *Help!* in the UK (Aug 13 in the US)

15 Aug The Beatles' second US tour opens at New York's Shea Stadium to a record audience of 55,600.

26 Oct The Beatles receive their MBEs at Buckingham Palace.

3 Dec UK album release of *Rubber Soul*. (Dec 6 in the US)

1966

4 Mar The *Evening Standard* publishes an interview with John, reported by Maureen Cleave, in which he states that the Beatles are "more popular than Jesus".

5 Aug Release of the album *Revolver*

6 Aug Brian Epstein holds a press conference in New York to explain John's "Jesus" comments.

11 Aug The Beatles fly to Chicago for the start of what is to prove their final US tour.

12 Aug Supported by the rest of the group, John faces the American Press to explain and apologize for his remarks.

29 Aug The Beatles make their last stage appearance at San Francisco's Candlestick Park.

5 Sept John goes to Celle in West Germany to begin filming his part in *How I Won the War*, where he is to acquire his trademark spectacles.

9 Nov John meets the conceptual artist Yoko Ono at her exhibition, Unfinished Paintings and Objects, at the Indica Gallery, London.

27 Nov John films a sketch for *Not Only...But Also*, to be broadcast on Christmas Day.

1967

17 Feb UK single release of "Strawberry Fields Forever"/ "Penny Lane."

26 May The Beatles' ground-breaking album *Sgt. Pepper's Lonely Hearts Club Band* is released ahead of the official date of 1 June..

25 Jun The Beatles perform "All You Need Is Love" on the world's first global satellite television link-up.

27 Aug Brian Epstein is found dead at home in bed, London.

11 Sept Shooting begins on The Beatles' next film, *Magical Mystery Tour*.

18 Oct *How I Won the War* premieres at the London Pavilion.

27 Nov Release of *Magical Mystery Tour* album in the US. In the UK, an EP of the same name is released on Dec 8)

1968

22 May John and Yoko Ono appear together in public for the first time, attending a party and Press conference for another Apple Boutique.

18 Jun John attends the opening of *In His Own Write* with Yoko, the play having been adapted by actor and friend, Victor Spinetti, from John's two books.

1 Jul You Are Here, John's first art exhibition, opens in London

22 Aug Cynthia sues John for divorce, on the grounds of his affair with Yoko Ono.

18 Oct A police raid on an apartment where John and Yoko are staying. The pair are charged with obstructing the police and with possession of cannabis.

8 Nov John and Cynthia are divorced.

22 Nov Release of *The Beatles (The White Album)*. Released Nov 25 in the US.

29 Nov John and Yoko's first album, *Unfinished Music No 1 - Two Virgins,* is released in the UK.

1969

13 Jan Release of the album *Yellow Submarine* in the UK (Jan 17 in the US).

30 Jan The Beatles perform together for the last time on the roof of the Apple building, London. The event is filmed as part of the *Let It Be* project.

20 Mar John and Yoko are married at the British Consulate in Gibraltar.

25 Mar John and Yoko begin a week-long "bed-in" at the Amsterdam Hilton, Holland.

9 May John and Yoko's second album, *Unfinished Music No 2 - Life With The Lions,* is released in the UK, on the newly formed Zapple label.

1 Jun "Give Peace a Chance" is recorded during the "bed-in" by The Plastic Ono Band, a makeshift group which includes John, Yoko and their friends, including guests such as Timothy Leary.

4 Jul John's first solo single, "Give Peace a Chance", is released, credited to The Plastic Ono Band.

26 Sept Release of the Beatles album *Abbey Road* (Oct 1 in the US).

13 Sept John decides to quit the Beatles whilst on his way to a hastily arranged concert in Toronto with The Plastic Ono Band; his decision, however is not made public.

24 Oct The Plastic Ono Band release "Cold Turkey" as a UK single.

7 Nov John and Yoko release their *Wedding Album* in the UK in a luxurious package.

13 Nov John Lennon offers a tiny island, Dornish, rent-free to a group of hippies.

12 Dec The Plastic Ono Band release the LP *Live Peace in Toronto,* worldwide.

1970

3/4 Jan Paul, George and Ringo record together for *Let It Be,* their last recording session in John's lifetime. John is absent.

15 Jan John's exhibition of lithographs, Bag One, opens in London.

6 Feb John and Yoko release "Instant Karma"/ "Who Has Seen The Wind?" in the UK.

10 Apr Paul publicly announces his resignation from the Beatles.

8 May Release of the album *Let It Be* (May 18 in the US)

11 Dec The LP John Lennon / The Plastic Ono Band is released worldwide.

1971

19 Feb The hearing to dissolve The Beatles & Co. Partnership commences in the London High Court.

12 Mar John and Yoko release "Power To The People"/ "Open Your Box" as a single in the UK.

Jul John records the album *Imagine,* mostly at his Tittenhurst Park home.

8 Oct The LP *Imagine* is released in the UK.

9-27 Oct John is a guest artist at Yoko's "This Is Not Here" exhibition in New York.

1 Dec "Happy Christmas (War Is Over)" is issued as a single in the US (November 24,. 1972 in the UK).

1972

12 Jun John and Yoko release their double LP, *Sometime In New York City* in the US (September 15 in the UK).

1973

Oct John embarks upon his "lost weekend", separating from Yoko and flying to LA with their secretary, May Pang.

Oct-Dec John records a rock and roll album produced by Phil Spector.

2 Nov US release of LP *Mind Games* and "Mind Games"/ "Meat City" single (November 16 in the UK).

1974

23 Sept John releases "Whatever Gets You Through The Night"/ "Beef Jerky" as a single in the US (Oct 4. in the UK).

26 Sept John releases his *Walls And Bridges* LP in the US (4th Oct. in the UK).

16 Nov John has his first US solo No.1 with "Whatever Gets You Through The Night."

16 Dec John issues "#9 Dream"/ "What You Got" as a US single (Jan 31 1975 in the UK).

6 Mar John issues a statement that his separation from Yoko is over.

10 Mar The single "Stand By Me"/ "Move Over Mrs L," is released in the US (Apr 18 in the UK).

13 Jun John gives his last performance before an audience, on *A Salute To Lew Grade,* television special.

7 Oct The deportation order which John has been fighting for some years, is reversed by the New York State Senate.

9 Oct Sean Taro Ono Lennon is born to John and Yoko on John's thirty-fifth Birthday.

24 Oct "Working Class Hero" is released in the UK only.

1976

26 Jan The Beatles recording contract with EMI expires, Paul stays with EMI, George and Ringo move to other labels, and John does not sign with anyone.

1 Apr John's father, Fred, dies in hospital in Brighton, England.

27 Jul John finally receives his Green Card.

Oct John decides to retire from music in order to focus on bringing up Sean.

1979

4 Aug John and Yoko begin studio work for a new album at the Hit Factory studio, Manhattan.

9 Sept John and Yoko begin a huge interview for *Playboy,* lasting almost three weeks.

22 Sept Yoko signs a recording contract for herself and John with the newly formed independent label, Geffen Records.

27 Oct John releases the single "(Just Like) Starting Over"/ "Kiss Kiss Kiss" in the US (Oct 24 in the UK).

17 Nov John and Yoko release the album *Double Fantasy.*

5 Dec John records an interview with *Rolling Stone* magazine.

8 Dec (Dec 9 in the UK) John is shot and killed outside the Dakota apartment building in New York.

10 Dec John is cremated at Hartsdale Crematorium, New York State.

14 Dec Ten minutes silence is observed around the world, at 7pm GMT, in memory of John.

14 Dec Extracts from the RKO interview are broadcast in the US.

20 Dec "(Just Like) Starting Over" goes to No.1 in the UK, having previously slipped down the charts from 8th to 21st position.

27 Dec "(Just Like) Starting Over" reaches the No.1 spot in the US, where it is to remain for five weeks. *Double Fantasy* tops the album chart.

1981

12 Jan US release of John's "Woman"/ "Beautiful Boy (Darling Boy)" (Jan 16 in the UK).

13 Mar US release of "Watching The Wheels"/ "Yes I'm Your Angel" (March 27 in the UK).

11 May George releases a tribute single, "All Those Years Ago," featuring Paul and Ringo, in the US (May 15 in the UK).

24 Aug John's murderer Mark Chapman is sentenced jailed for a minimum term of twenty years, and a maximum of life imprisonment.

1982

24 Feb Yoko and Sean attend the Grammy awards, collecting the best album award for *Double Fantasy.*

15 Nov EMI release "Love" as a single.

1984

19 Jan US album release of John and Yoko's 'Milk And Honey' (Jan 23 in the UK).

21 Mar Yoko officially opens the Strawberry Fields site in Central Park with Julian, Sean and mayor Ed Koch.

Acknowledgments

The photographs in this book are from the archives of Associated Newspapers. Particular thanks to the photographers' collective work over the last 45 years. Thanks also to Steve Torrington, Alan Pinnock, Katie Lee, Dave Sheppard, Brian Jackson, Richard Jones and all the present staff at Associated Newspapers.

Additional photographs by Getty Images: 10, 11, 12, 14, 16, 22, 24, 107, 113, 115, 117, 118, 124, 128, 134, 148, 168, 172, 194, 206, 209, 210, 212, 213, 220.

Thanks also to Cliff Salter and John Dunne.